Sports Fundamentals Series

WEIGHT TRAINING
Fundamentals

David Sandler

Human Kinetics

Library of Congress Cataloging-in-Publication Data

Human Kinetics Publishers.
  Weight training fundamentals / Human Kinetics with David Sandler.
    p.   cm.
  ISBN 0-7360-4488-4 (soft cover)
    1. Weight training.   I. Sandler, David.   II. Title.
  GV546.3 .S26   2003
  796.41--dc21   2002015222

ISBN: 0-7360-4488-4

Acquisitions Editor: Ed McNeely; **Developmental Editor:** Cynthia McEntire; **Assistant Editor:** John Wentworth; **Copyeditor:** Barb Field; **Proofreader:** Sarah Wiseman; **Graphic Designer:** Robert Reuther; **Graphic Artist:** Francine Hamerski; **Photo and Art Manager:** Dan Wendt; **Cover Designer:** Keith Blomberg; **Photographer (cover and interior):** Dan Wendt; **Mac Illustrator:** Roberto Sabas; **Medical Illustrator:** Katharine Galasyn-Wright; **Printer:** Versa Press

Many thanks to the Mettler Center, Champaign, Illinois, for the use of their facilities.

Human Kinetics books are available at special discounts for bulk purchase. Special editions or book excerpts can also be created to specification. For details, contact the Special Sales Manager at Human Kinetics.

Printed in the United States of America   10 9 8 7 6 5 4 3 2 1

Human Kinetics
Web site: http://www.HumanKinetics.com/

United States: Human Kinetics
P.O. Box 5076
Champaign, IL 61825-5076
800-747-4457
e-mail: humank@hkusa.com

Canada: Human Kinetics
475 Devonshire Road Unit 100
Windsor, ON N8Y 2L5
800-465-7301 (in Canada only)
e-mail: orders@hkcanada.com

Europe: Human Kinetics
107 Bradford Road
Stanningley
Leeds LS28 6AT, United Kingdom
+44 (0) 113 255 5665
e-mail: hk@hkeurope.com

Australia: Human Kinetics
57A Price Avenue
Lower Mitcham, South Australia 5062
08 8277 1555
e-mail: liahka@senet.com.au

New Zealand: Human Kinetics
P.O. Box 105-231, Auckland Central
09-523-3462
e-mail: hkp@ihug.co.nz

Welcome to Sports Fundamentals

The Sports Fundamentals Series uses a learn-by-doing approach to teach those who want to play, not just read. Clear, concise instructions and illustrations make it easy to become more proficient in the game or activity, allowing readers to participate quickly and have more fun.

Between the covers, this book contains rock-solid information, precise directions, and clear photos and illustrations that immerse you in the heart of the sport or activity. Each fundamental chapter is divided into four major sections:

- **You Can Do It!:** Jump right into the activity with a clear explanation of how to perform an essential skill.
- **More to Choose and Use:** Find out more about the skill or learn exciting alternatives.
- **Take It to the Gym:** Apply the new skill with a focus on safety and effectiveness.
- **Give It a Go:** Place the new skill within a training program that gets results.

No more sitting on the bench! The Sports Fundamentals Series gets you right into the middle of things. Apply the techniques as they are learned, and have fun.

Contents

Welcome to Weight Training

Good, you've chosen to begin a weight training program. You've made the right move by choosing to do it properly. When exercises are performed correctly, resistance training can have terrific results, such as increasing strength, power, and muscular endurance; improving balance and coordination; and decreasing body fat. When poor technique is used, however, or no attention is paid to proper form, resistance training can lead to injury.

Resistance training has inherent qualities that make it next to impossible to see results quickly. This is a good thing. You will need to put forth an effort and plan your workouts intelligently. Success depends on your interest, and your interest depends on your enjoyment. With the information in this book, you will be able to design and implement the perfect training program.

Sets and Repetitions

Behind every good training program is the proper execution of an exercise. This first concept—proper execution—is the starting point for all routines. The repetition—the execution of a movement in both directions—is the foundation for improvement and the basis for each exercise. A single repetition (rep, for short) consists of an eccentric contraction in which the muscle lengthens and a concentric contraction in which the muscle shortens.

Performing repetitions in succession without a break between them is considered a set of repetitions. However, what truly defines a set is the break taken between each grouping of consecutive repetitions. To set up an exercise program, you need to define the number of sets of a certain exercise you will execute. Within each set, you determine the number of reps based on the goal of the training routine. Rep and set notation is written as Y sets × Z reps. For example, 3 × 10 means three sets of 10 repetitions.

Before you begin to exercise, however, you need to understand that the manner in which you perform reps will have an impact on how your muscle develops. Probably the single most important thing to remember is that every rep needs to be done properly. For success, you must strive to execute the perfect rep on each and every attempt. This prevents you from developing bad lifting habits, reduces your chances of injury, and improves your chances of developing quality musculature.

For the perfect rep, use two to three seconds to raise the weight and three to four seconds to lower it. Eliminate all unnecessary movements, including excessive swinging, to prevent cheating. The weight should be light enough for you to handle properly for the prescribed number of reps.

So how many sets and reps should you perform? Training can be done many ways, and no one method is necessarily better than the next. The following guidelines will help you decide what you need.

In general, the prescription is one to three sets of 8 to 12 repetitions. Muscle responds well to repeated stimulus within this range. However, on occasion it may be best to do only 5 reps, or you might want to do 20 or more. As the weight increases, the number of attainable reps decreases. More strength is required to move heavier weights, and you must improve your strength first.

Lifting lighter weight allows you to complete more repetitions, improving your ability to perform for a longer duration. The general rule is that lighter weight and more repetitions improves muscular endurance, whereas heavier weight and fewer reps increases strength. For beginners, I recommend using lighter weights and working to complete about 12 repetitions. As you become more accustomed to the rigors of weightlifting, you may choose to use more or fewer reps.

The number of sets depends on your ability to recover within each set. Typically, the harder you work within the set, the harder it is to complete more sets. A general recommendation of one to three sets, with two or three being optimal, is the way to go. Avoid doing too many sets, whether you are a beginner or expert. A single set of exercise produces significant results. More is not better; the number of sets depends greatly on the quality of the repetitions. Improvement comes from the number of quality sets, not just the number of sets.

Recovery is an important part of weight training. How long should you rest between sets? It may be obvious, but the harder you work, the longer you need to recover. The length of time you rest influences the number of reps you will be able to do and the overall number of sets you can complete. A good general rule is to rest 60 to 90 seconds between sets. A shorter rest period (say 30 seconds) develops muscle endurance more and also requires a lighter weight. A longer rest time (three minutes or more) means you will develop a greater amount of strength and be able to handle more weight in subsequent sets.

To develop your program, you need to establish the number of sets and reps and the amount of rest you will take so that you can achieve the results you want. The table classifies general goals and approximate lifting criteria.

WEIGHT TRAINING GOALS AND LIFTING SPECIFICATIONS

Goal	Sets	Reps	Weight	Rest (sec)
Muscular endurance	1 to 3	15 to 25	Light	30 to 60
	2 to 5	10 to 15	Light	15 to 45
Muscular strength	1 to 4	5 to 8	Heavy	60 to 180
				90 to 210
General fitness	1 to 4	8 to 12	Medium to heavy	60 to 120

Proper Technique

Using proper lifting technique is very important. Each chapter will explain the proper technique for the exercise described, but we need to discuss the rep execution itself. A properly executed rep consists of moving the weight through a joint's entire range of motion.

Each joint in your body (such as the elbow) can move through a certain range before either bone contacts bone or muscle contacts muscle. *Flexion* describes the decrease in a joint angle, and *extension* describes the increase in a joint angle. For example, when your arms are down at your sides, your elbow is fully extended; when you bend your elbows to make your biceps bulge, your arms are fully flexed. At the fully extended position, your arm cannot open any more because the bones of the upper and lower arm hit each other. At the fully flexed position, the biceps makes contact with the forearm.

Proper lifting technique requires you to perform reps throughout the full range of motion, unless you are injured. Cheat reps or shortened-range reps inevitably will decrease overall muscle involvement and decrease your muscle's ability to grow evenly. The shape of your muscle, while mostly genetic, is partially determined by the performance of each rep.

Weight Training Principles

If you are to derive any "real" benefits from training, you need to understand the underlying principles of weight training. These principles provide guideance and a foundation for any well-designed training program.

FITT

The FITT principle—the acronym stands for frequency, intensity, time, and type—has already been discussed in terms of exercise performance. Earlier we looked at the number of sets and reps (frequency), the relative weight (intensity), and the rest (time) between sets. Let's not forget that the number of times you work out per week, the length of the workouts, and the number of different exercises performed will also play a role in an appropriate program.

On average, your workout should last no more than one hour, and you should choose 10 to 12 exercises per workout. Training three times a week is ideal; however, any number of times a week is better than no times per week. Although a more advanced lifter may train four or five times a week, it is important to respect your body's ability to recover. Take at least 24 and preferably 48 hours of rest between workouts training the same body areas.

The final "T" is for type of exercise. As you will see when you get into the exercises, you can use a variety of equipment, such as dumbbells, plate weight barbells, and machines.

Gradual Progressive Overload

The overload principle states that the body must receive a stimulus greater than it is used to for it to gain any major benefits. That doesn't mean the body will not benefit from using a lesser stimulus; however, greater adaptation takes place when the stress is "larger" than normal. Overload can be in the form of increasing the resistance (or intensity level), duration (length of time) of activity, frequency of activity, and type of activity, or a combination of any of those.

Now wait a moment. Don't just rush off to the gym, load up the bar with a ton of weight, and try to lift it. Remember, your body isn't prepared to handle a lot of weight, especially if you are a beginner. The principle of progression says to start gradually and add a little to each workout. That means either increasing the weight used by a small amount (usually 5 to 10 pounds) or trying to perform a few more reps (with perfect form, of course). The decision to increase either weight or reps depends on your desired outcome.

It is extremely important to progress slowly. The most common reason for injury is progressing too fast. Before you make any increase in your workout, be sure that you have truly mastered the previous weight and are ready to move on. The combination of progression and overload leads to the principle known as gradual progressive overload (GPO).

Individuality and Specificity

Okay, so you're ready now. Or are you? Let's say you want to go exercise with your buddy. Is he or she the same age, height, weight, and build as you? If not, then you must realize that there will be some differences in the weights you use, the performance of the exercise, and the benefits you each receive. This difference is known as individuality.

The principle of individuality simply recognizes that everyone is different and that exercise programs should be designed with these differences in mind. Before you begin to exercise, you need to understand that everyone has different physical attributes, abilities, interests, motivations, and improvement rates. All of these factors should be considered when developing a training routine.

Well, now that you know how to do it, you need to know what to do. The body will respond and make improvements that are specific to the type of stimulus placed on it. This is called the specificity principle. In other words, to see specific results, you need to exercise using equipment and techniques that target the muscle you want to develop or the sport-specific skill you want to improve.

The body is an amazing piece of machinery. It responds to how it is treated. Muscles will experience increases and decreases according to how they are or are not trained. Individual muscles or groups of muscles adapt specifically to the type of training done. For example, if you want to increase the size of your biceps muscle, you should do arm curls. Although this sounds almost ridiculously commonsense, it is often not practiced in the weight room. If you walk into the typical weight room, you will see people doing all kinds of crazy things. This activity violates the principle of specificity. If the naked eye can't see a direct benefit from an exercise, then there probably isn't one.

You need to design a program that makes efficient use of your time and zeros in on your goals. Weight training should not be a

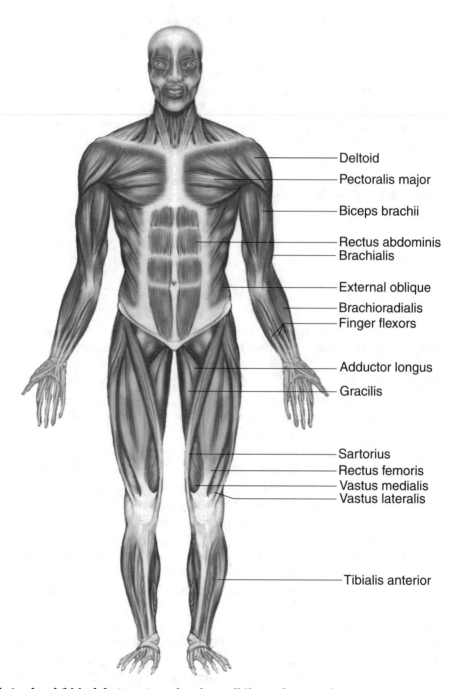

Deltoid
Pectoralis major
Biceps brachii
Rectus abdominis
Brachialis
External oblique
Brachioradialis
Finger flexors
Adductor longus
Gracilis
Sartorius
Rectus femoris
Vastus medialis
Vastus lateralis
Tibialis anterior

A good weight training program develops all the major muscles.

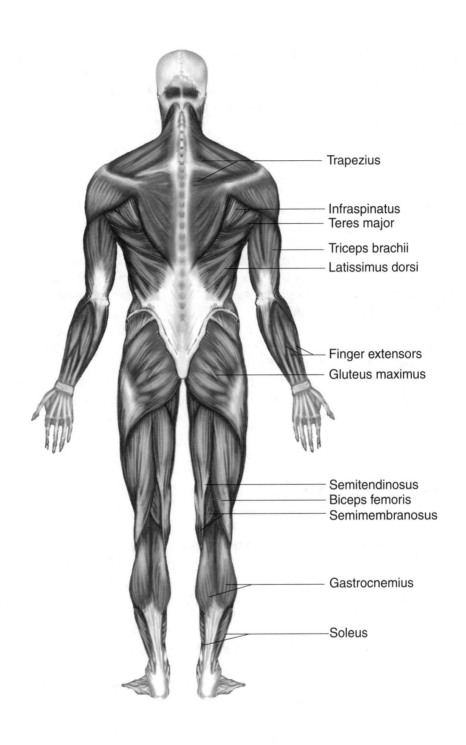

Trapezius

Infraspinatus
Teres major

Triceps brachii
Latissimus dorsi

Finger extensors
Gluteus maximus

Semitendinosus
Biceps femoris
Semimembranosus

Gastrocnemius

Soleus

mystery. Nor is there a single secret to success. Smart lifting means good results. The recommended exercise prescription is two to three sets of 8 to 12 repetitions of 10 to 12 different exercises emphasizing all of the major muscle groups: shoulders, chest, back, arms, abs, glutes, and legs.

Adaptation

Finally, we need to discuss adaptation, a term frequently used in discussing weight training. Your body will adapt to anything you do. Unfortunately, this is why people gain weight and lose strength and flexibility when they do nothing. You have a great chance right now to help yourself for the rest of your life. Resistance training offers long-term, lifelong benefits. You can expect improvement in muscle strength and endurance, increases in muscle size, stronger bones, and improvement in your overall appearance and feeling of well-being. Lifting weights will even help you burn more fat. Your body will make these specific adaptations in response to your properly progressed weight training routine.

Now that you are armed with the basic components of a training program and understand the fundamental principles that go along with it, we need to clarify a few more items before you can start your workout.

Clothing and Equipment

The great thing about weight training is that you don't need to rush off to the store to buy new clothes the way you would for a wedding. Except for a few guidelines, pretty much anything goes. Wear loose, comfortable clothing to permit easy movement, improve range of motion, and increase overall comfort. A good pair of shoes will absorb pressure at the ankle, knee, and lower back during leg work and standing exercises. Although rings may keep people away from you, they will pinch the finger, possibly causing blisters. Make sure your jewelry cannot get caught in any moving parts of the machines you use.

A pair of gloves that fit well will prevent the development of calluses. Not wearing gloves will force your hands to toughen up against the bar's knurly surface. Gloves serve no other functional purpose in weight training.

Dumbbell Variations

There are likely hundreds of variations of the major exercises presented in this book. One of the easiest and more productive ways to add variety to your workout is to use dumbbells. Unlike weight machines, dumbbells can be used anywhere. They are available in nearly every gym and can even be used in your home.

The movements are the same when you use dumbbells except each arm is free to move in its own path. This means two things. First, you must use good technique to keep the dumbbells following the proper path. Second, you can alter your arm position so that the movement will be more comfortable. For example, in the bench press your palms could be turned toward each other instead of facing in the same direction, if that is an easier grip for you.

Remember, when you use dumbbells, the stabilization normally provided by the weight machine or barbell must be provided by you. Decrease the weight and get control of the dumbbells before you try the tricky stuff.

Avoid using wrist straps, knee wraps, and belts. These devices tend to prevent strengthening of the wrists, knees, and trunk. When extra support is given to weak joint areas, those areas do not develop the strength they need. A crutch is only needed when you have an injury; otherwise you will not benefit from its use. True, the initial few workouts will potentially make your wrists and knees sore, but this will also be the time when you strengthen them to withstand further stresses.

Quite interesting and generally unknown is that a belt serves as a wall for the abdominal muscles to press against. This raises the pressure in your trunk and forces your lower back to stabilize. It is not designed to give your back something to press against. Although weak abdominals is the reason most often cited for using belts, the longer you use a belt, the longer it will take to strengthen your back and abdominals. Having said that, it is advisable to use a belt when lifting very heavy weights to ensure that you have enough support. But for routines using light to moderate weights, a belt is not necessary.

Now you have the right clothes and shoes. Your gloves are on. Before you hoist that first barbell, however, you need to prepare your body for action. In chapter 1, you will learn about warming up, cooling down, and stretching. All three elements are vital to a good exercise program.

Warm Up, Stretch, and Cool Down

The warm-up is vital for reducing injuries. More important, it prepares the body for the task ahead. Take a short walk, ride a bike, or jog for 5 to 10 minutes before weight training. This helps prepare the body to increase oxygen intake and gets the blood flowing to the muscles. Warm up at a slow pace, but work hard enough to break a mild sweat. A well-designed program begins with a 10-minute warm-up on a bicycle, treadmill, or stair climber followed by 10 to 20 minutes of good stretching before resistance training or aerobic training.

After working out, take the time to cool down. The cool-down increases the body's ability to return to normal after exercise by preventing the blood from pooling in certain areas. The cool-down is similar to the warm-up. Perform 5 to 10 minutes of a slow, rhythmic exercise, followed by 10 minutes of a full-body stretching routine.

Are You Double Jointed?

The term *double jointed* only means that someone has a large range of motion within a joint. No one really has two joints in one place. Generally, a double-jointed person is able to hyperextend a joint without someone else's help, causing an exaggerated stretch of the muscle and joint. In most cases (though there are exceptions), everyone has the same number of joints.

Stretch after performing a good warm-up or cool-down. Never stretch a cold muscle. Before any type of activity, a good stretch will help the muscles get ready. Not only does stretching prepare the muscles to work, it is also a good indicator of residual soreness or injury. If stretching causes sharp pain, or if you cannot stretch as far as usual, then avoid exercising that muscle group.

Always stretch all muscles before and after exercise, whether or not that muscle group is being trained. Often a muscle will tighten up or spasm in a part of the body other than the area being trained, causing discomfort. For example, the hamstrings may cramp up while the lifter performs an unrelated muscle group bench press. Cramping in an area not being worked often occurs during weight lifting because, as the body strains to lift the weight, muscles other than those directly involved in the lift tighten up to help the body create the necessary force.

During a stretch, the muscle is elongated past its normal resting length. This loosens up the muscle, which has become tight during rest. Stretching helps prevent the muscle from cramping or tightening.

The three major types of stretches are static, dynamic, and ballistic. Ballistic stretching is used by athletes and advanced lifters, but beginners should avoid it. In ballistic stretching, the stretcher uses a bouncing motion to move from an unstretched position to a stretched position. Ballistic stretching is only used in specific training programs and should be attempted only with supervision.

In static stretching, you move to a joint's maximum range and hold the stretch for 6 to 10 seconds or longer. In dynamic stretching, you take 10 to 20 seconds to move from an unstretched position to the maximum stretched position. Both static and dynamic stretching increase the joint's range of motion over time. Both types can be used in a general fitness program.

The main muscle groups that need to be considered in a stretching routine are the quadriceps, hamstrings, groin (adductors and abductors), lower back, triceps, and pectoralis (pecs). Secondary areas include the calves (especially if you jog), neck, shins, biceps, forearms, upper back (latissimus dorsi), and the joints of the ankle, wrists, knees, and shoulders. Ideally, you should stretch all muscles every day. However, if time is limited, stretching only the primary muscles is fine. Be sure to stretch muscles you are training both before and after your workout.

A good warm-up stretching routine does not need to take long, but it must incorporate all the major muscle groups in the body. Whether you use static or dynamic stretching, the routine should take only 10 minutes at the most. Before stretching an injured area, consult your physician; stretching and exercising an injured area may not be wise.

Weight Training and Flexibility

Flexibility is usually defined as the range of motion within a joint or group of joints in a system. This definition is somewhat inadequate, however. Joint range is based on bone shape and the stretch and pliability of connective tissues (tendons and ligaments).

Although part of your ability to be flexible is genetic, you can become more flexible through a dedicated, regular routine of stretches. Stretching slowly increases the range of motion within the joint.

Contrary to popular belief, weight training does not reduce flexibility as long as you stretch before each session. Weight training works in several ways to help increase flexibility. It increases muscle strength and prevents injury by increasing the tendon's ability to stretch as well as increasing its strength, which prevents tearing. Strength training also helps increase the tendon's ability to return to its normal shape after deformation. (Think of a rubber band that, over time, loses its ability to return to its original shape after being stretched. Weight training keeps tendons pliable over time so they return to their resting length after being stretched.)

Strength training will help you bring the area of the body being stretched into position and hold the position. Without muscle strength and endurance, you can't hold the position as long. The most important safety benefit is that weight training increases the strength of the connective tissues (cartilage, ligaments, and tendons). This prevents tears and overrotation or dislocation of a joint. Strength training decreases the chances of injury during flexibility training, but remember, no form of training can prevent all injuries.

CALF STRETCH

Lean forward against a wall with your legs in lunge position. Bend your front leg and place your weight on it. Stretch the back of your back leg, keeping your back heel on the ground. This stretch also stretches the hip flexors.

QUAD STRETCH

You can do this stretch either standing or lying on your stomach. Bend your knee and grab your ankle, pulling your heel to your buttocks. For an advanced stretch for your rectus femoris and hip flexors, pull your leg back during the stretch.

HAMSTRING AND LOWER BACK STRETCH

Sit on the ground with one leg extended and the other bent, the bottom of your foot touching the knee of your extended leg. This is the modified hurdler position. Reach toward the foot of your extended leg, tucking your head down. For an additional calf stretch, grab hold of the toes of your extended leg and pull back on them as you stretch forward.

GROIN STRETCH

Sit on the ground with the bottoms of your feet touching each other. Press your knees down with your elbows as you pull your heels toward your groin.

HIP FLEXOR STRETCH

This is an advanced stretch. Kneel on the ground with one knee on the ground and the other knee bent with the foot flat. Lean toward the front leg. Keep the upper body upright or even slightly backward. For added stretch, press your hands against the knee, pushing your upper body backward.

PEC STRETCH

Stand in a doorway or next to a machine. Raise your arms, bending your elbows. Lean into the doorway or toward the machine.

TRICEPS STRETCH

Raise your arm overhead, flex your elbow, and reach down your back. Use your other arm to pull back on the elbow for additional stretch.

REAR DELTOID AND UPPER BACK STRETCH

Reach across your body at chest height with one arm. Grab that arm at the elbow with your other hand and continue to pull your arm across your chest.

UPPER BACK STRETCH

Stand upright about three feet in front of a pole or machine. Reach out and grab the pole or machine with both hands, bending at the waist. Press down on the the pole or machine, stretching your upper back. This will also stretch your pecs.

BICEPS STRETCH

Fully extend your arm out in front with your palm and forearm turned up. With your other hand, grab the hand of the outstretched arm and gently pull back on your fingers.

Chest

One of the most noticeable parts of the body, the chest is responsible for many arm movements such as throwing, pushing, and hitting. A strong, well-defined chest is the hallmark of a great training program. The major chest muscles are the pectoralis major and pectoralis minor. These strong muscles move the arms across the body and toward the waist. The pecs allow for several different movements, and there are several different ways to strengthen them.

The main lift, and perhaps the single most practiced exercise, is the bench press. No other exercise is more heralded than this spectacle of strength and prowess. The bench press works not only the pecs, but several other muscles. In addition to developing the chest, the bench press helps develop many of the muscles that act on the shoulder joint, including the anterior deltoid and the triceps.

Bench Press

The motion of the bench press resembles an upside-down push-up. This exercise requires a great deal of concentration and arm coordination. It is important that you follow proper technique and start with a weight you can handle.

Lie on the weight bench. Grab the bar, hands shoulder-width or a little wider apart. Keep your feet on the floor. If the bench is too high for your feet to reach the floor, you can put your feet on the bench with your heels against your buttocks or place weight plates or blocks under your feet. Keep your shoulders, buttocks, and head against the bench at all times. To relieve the pressure on your lower back, it should have a slight arch. You should be able to slide your hand under your lower back.

Inhale deeply and remove the bar from the bench. Pause a moment, then begin to lower the weight toward your chest. Lower the bar steadily, and pause for a moment when it touches your chest. The bar should cross at or slightly above your nipples.

Starting position.

Lower the weight.

To begin the ascent, rapidly "drive" the weight up, maintaining a constant speed. Exhale as you lift the weight. The bar will naturally follow an arc and end up just over your neck. Continue to lift the weight until your arms are fully extended. Although many people feel locking the arms is bad, it is important to move the bar through the complete range of motion. A gentle lock is acceptable and ensures that you have completed the upward motion.

There are several variations of the bench press and many other chest exercises. Each exercise works the pecs and supporting muscles slightly differently. Remember, specificity requires that you choose exercises that reflect your needs and goals.

Pause at the chest.

Lift the weight.

Incline Press

The incline press works the upper pecs a little more than the flat bench press, especially the middle shoulder and triceps. Set the bench at about a 45-degree angle. Decreasing the angle puts more emphasis on the middle chest and front shoulders; increasing the angle puts more emphasis on the upper chest and middle shoulders. Lower and raise the weight as you did in the bench press. The bar should touch a little higher on your chest, near your collarbone.

Incline press.

Dumbbell Bench Press

This movement emphasizes the muscles that help stabilize the shoulder. The weights will feel awkward when you do the dumbbell bench for the first time. Controlling them is the key. Lie on your back on a flat bench. Dig your shoulders into the bench and pull your shoulder blades together. This tightens your body, lending additional support to the shoulders. Start with the arms fully extended, a dumbbell in each hand, palms turned out. Lower the dumbbells to your chest, moving your elbows away from your body. Press the dumbbells back to the starting position. If you feel the dumbbells getting squirrelly on you, try to bring the dumbbells together when you return them to the starting position.

Dumbbell bench press.

Machine Pec Fly

The pec fly is another exercise that isolates the pecs. It allows for greater range of motion than the bench press. The pec fly can be performed with dumbbells or a machine. With the machine fly, the arms are extended out to the sides at chest height with the elbows bent 90 degrees. The pads usually rest against the elbows. Apply equal force to both pads as you squeeze your elbows toward each other. In the fully contracted position, the elbows touch (or nearly touch).

Machine pec fly.

Dumbbell Pec Fly

The dumbbell pec fly is more difficult than the machine pec fly. Lie on a flat weight bench with your arms fully extended over your chest. With the dumbbells in your hands, turn your palms inward and touch the dumbbells. Keeping a slight bend in your elbows, pull the dumbbells apart until your arms are parallel to the ground. Pause briefly at the bottom position. Using a bear-hugging motion, return the dumbbells to the top.

Dumbbell pec fly.

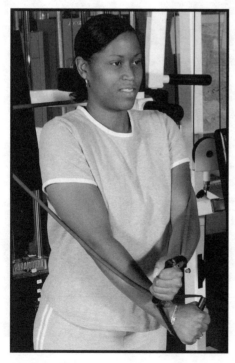

Cable cross.

Cable Cross

Perhaps the most flamboyant of chest exercises is the cable cross. The cable cross is a good way to work the pecs and can be performed one arm at a time. Stand in the middle of the cable machine with arms extended to the sides at shoulder height. Grab the machine handles, palms down, and pull toward the middle of your body, keeping your elbows slightly bent. Keep a slight bend in your knees and lean slightly forward. Cross palms about 6 to 12 inches in front of your belly button.

Train Smart

Veteran bench pressers know a few tricks for successful benching. The ultimate goal, especially for men, is to load up the plates, trying to hit the legendary three-plate pinnacle (three 45-pound plates per side, plus the 45-pound bar, totaling 315 pounds). Although that may not be in your sights now, it may be in your future. Don't try to lift like the veterans until your technique is solid and you have developed sufficient strength.

Grip all barbells and dumbbells in a monkey grip, with your thumb wrapped around the bar or dumbbell. Generally, a narrow grip involves the triceps more, whereas a wider grip involves more of the pecs.

The key to good technique is to get into a solid, tight position on the bench. Keep your body in contact with the bench throughout the entire pressing movement. Use your feet for support; placing them on the bench reduces stability and decreases the emphasis on the working muscles. Position your feet a little wider than shoulder-width apart and slightly back. Pull your shoulders back to form a solid base, and keep them in check throughout the movement.

Control the descent of the weight. A controlled descent allows the muscles to build up elastic energy that will help lift the bar back up. As you begin to drive the weight up, push your body back into the bench and flatten your shoulders. Don't bounce the weight off your chest or use momentum to move the weight, as this can lead to injury and loss of control.

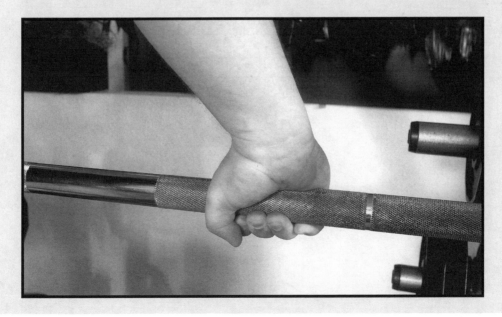

CREATE A CHEST ROUTINE

The bench press is a great stand-alone exercise, but when it's combined with other exercises, you can reach new levels in chest development. The bench press is easily coupled with the pec fly. To show your pecs who's boss, try the pre- or postexhaust training routines. Simply perform a set of pec flys immediately before (preexhaust) or after (postexhaust) the bench press. Allow only enough rest between exercises to move to the next exercise.

For additional variety, try alternating between exercises within your workout or within your training week. For example, perform flat bench presses one workout and incline bench presses the next. Perform cable crosses between bench presses and incline presses. The combinations are limited only by your imagination. The bench press incorporates so many muscles that you are bound to work your chest well. Remember, muscles will begin to tire when you perform multiple sets of several exercises. Adjust your weights accordingly.

Don't be afraid to change things. You don't always have to start with the bench press on Monday. Try one of the popular combinations shown in the table. Routine 1 is good for general fitness, routine 2 is appropriate for strength development, and routine 3 is a good change of pace.

WORK THE CHEST

Routine 1	Routine 2	Routine 3
Bench press 2 × 10	Bench press 3 × 8	Pec fly 1 × 8
Incline press 2 × 10	Cable cross 2 × 8	Bench press 1 × 8
Pec fly 2 × 10	Incline press 3 × 8	Repeat pec fly and bench press two more times Incline press 1 × 12

Upper Back

One important strategy for weight training is to balance your muscle building to prevent orthopedic problems. Therefore, while training the chest, it is essential to train the back as well. Upper back exercises involve pulling movements. In all pulling movements, the latissimus dorsi (lats), rhomboids, trapezius (traps), rear deltoids, and teres major are worked, as well as the biceps and other arm flexors. In fact, many routines incorporate both upper back and biceps work on the same day. When working the back, concentrate on initiating all movements with the back muscles and not the biceps. Biceps involvement is inevitable, however, and must be considered when developing your program.

The core movement for the upper back is the seated row, the perfect complement to the bench press. Proper execution of this lift will not only help with anchoring a tug-of-war contest, but will improve your overall upper body shape.

Seated Row

The seated row can be done on a traditional machine or a cable machine. Here we will focus on the cable machine exercise.

Your initial hand position will dictate which muscles you emphasize. With your arms beside you and your elbows in close, you will emphasize the lat muscles slightly more. If your elbows are out to the sides (armpits forming a 90-degree angle), you will place greater emphasis on the rear deltoids and rhomboids. In either case, all muscles are worked in every position, and the actual movement itself remains the same.

Concentrate on your body position. Get yourself properly set in the machine. Make sure your form is tight. Since the cable machine provides no support for your upper body, you must keep your body positioned correctly. Look forward and sit up tall. Contract your abs, and do not bend at the waist.

Starting position.

Sit upright with your chest out. The handles should be at arm's length when your arms are completely extended. Grab the handles and slowly pull them to your chest.

During the movement, pull your shoulder blades together. Pull back as far as you can, then pause momentarily. Do not use the momentum created by bending at your waist to pull the handles back.

Return the weight to the starting position by slowly allowing the weight to extend your arms. Fight against the resistance as your arms extend.

Pull weight to chest.

Dumbbell Row

Rest your left hand and knee on a flat bench, in line about two feet apart. Use your right leg to keep your balance. Keep a straight back, eyes looking at the ground. Do not raise your head. Grab the dumbbell with your right hand, arm extended. Pull up and back, fixing your elbow tight to your right side. The motion is similar to sawing wood. Slowly extend your right arm, returning the dumbbell to the starting position. Do not jerk the weight up or rotate the body during the lift. If this happens, you are lifting too much weight.

Dumbbell row.

Lat Pulldown

The primary variation of the seated row is the lat pulldown, which—you guessed it—works the lats. Sit in a lat pulldown machine with your arms extended overhead. Hold the bar in a monkey grip, hands about twice shoulder-width apart, palms turned away from you. Your arms should form a V overhead. Lean slightly back from the waist to prevent hitting yourself in the head with the bar. Bring the bar down to the top of your chest. Return the bar to the starting position. Some lifters pull the bar behind their head, but this position often compromises the upper neck and causes the lower back to round. Both are major flaws. If you choose to pull the bar behind your head, maintain proper position by keeping your chest up and your head facing forward.

Lat pulldown.

Chin-up.

Chin-Up

Another variation is the chin-up. If you have trouble performing chin-ups using your body weight, try the front pull. The exercises are similar; the only difference is whether your body is anchored to the machine or the bar is anchored to the machine. For the chin-up, hang from a chin-up bar, arms fully extended, palms turned toward you. Your elbows should be in direct line with your shoulders. Your hands should grip the bar about shoulder-width apart. Pull the bar past your chin to the top of your chest. Slowly lower your body to the starting point. If you have trouble lifting your body weight, then perform front pulls. Work on full range of motion, and in time, you will be able to chin your body.

Front Pull

If you have trouble chinning your body, try the front pull on a lat pulldown machine. Sit in the machine. Grab the overhead bar, arms fully extended, palms turned toward you, hands about shoulder-width apart. Pull the bar past your chin.

Front pull.

Dumbbell Pullover

Another great exercise is the pullover. The dumbbell pullover requires paying strict attention to form. Stand a dumbbell on end at one end of a weight bench. Lie on the bench with your head at the end near the dumbbell. Reach back and grab the dumbbell with both hands, elbows slightly bent. Pull the dumbbell over your face. For obvious reasons, it is wise to have a firm grip on the dumbbell. The dumbbell will track in an arc from the floor to a position over your face. Keep your arms extended with elbows slightly bent. Do not flex and extend your elbow during the movement. This is an isolation movement; the only joint that should move is the shoulder.

Dumbbell pullover.

Earn Your Wings

Lifters who have exceptionally large, flared out, V-shaped lats are said to have "bat wings," referring to the way a bat's wings flare to the side. To truly develop bat wings, focus on your back. A trick used by many lifters is to retract the scapula (pull the shoulder blades together) prior to initiating the movement. By doing this, you not only involve the tough-to-work rhomboids, but you position the lats so that they bear the load more evenly and decrease biceps involvement. Concentrate on initiating the movement with your upper back.

Proper alignment is very important. Keep your chest up and your head facing forward. Looking down or up will cause your back to round and involve other muscles in the lift, decreasing the overall contribution of the back muscles. Getting into a tight position—maintaining good posture, limiting extraneous movement, and keeping control—for any lift is essential. The back is no exception.

Remember that when working the upper back, the lower back must constantly support the movement. To perform exercises correctly, maintain proper back alignment. Stick your chest out and keep your chin up—this will keep the lower back from rounding. Do not initiate upper back exercises with the lower back. Often lifters perform seated cable rows by leaning forward at the waist. This action prevents the lats and other back muscles from working through the entire range of motion. Using the lower back and biceps to gain momentum during seated rows takes the work off the latissimus dorsi and decreases the rate of development.

Once you have worked up to heavier weights, using straps to hold onto the bar is fine if you do not care about developing grip strength and forearm musculature. The straps will help you lift more weight, but usually at the expense of proper form. By allowing your grip strength to develop, not only will you improve your overall pulling strength (which is more applicable for sport performance), but your rate of progression will be more even. Remember the principle of progression; you sacrifice form and development when you try to progress too quickly.

give it a go

BUILD YOUR BACK

Since the back is a critical body part, it should be exercised on its own as much as possible. Although you can't completely eliminate the biceps from back work, you can reduce their contribution by concentrating on using the back muscles to begin each movement. Use slow, deliberate movements. Jerking the weight will activate the biceps first and may lead to grip fatigue.

One practical way to accomplish a complete back workout is to use a variety of pulls in your program. I recommend incorporating both the seated row and the lat pulldown into your workouts. A great way to target the back muscles from every angle is to perform fewer sets of each individual exercise but include more exercises. For a real challenge, try using the pullover in a pre- or postexhaust routine with the lat pulldown (sample routine 3).

WORK THE BACK

Routine 1	Routine 2	Routine 3
Seated row 3 $\times$ 10	Seated row 2 $\times$ 8	Pullover 1 $\times$ 10
Lat pulldown 3 $\times$ 10	Lat pulldown 2 $\times$ 8 Front pull 2 $\times$ 8	Lat pulldown 1 $\times$ 10 Repeat pullover and lat pulldown two more times Seated row 2 $\times$ 12

Shoulders

The deltoids are actually three distinct muscles with three different functions. The anterior (front) deltoid raises your arm to the front of your body and pulls your arm across your body. The medial (middle) deltoid moves your arm out away from the side of your body. The posterior (rear) deltoid primarily pulls your arm back. The deltoids work in concert with the rotator cuff, a collective name that describes four small, deep muscles that hold the shoulders in place. These muscles allow the arm to rotate at the shoulder. When improper technique is used or the shoulder is overused, the muscles of the rotator cuff are often the ones that feel it.

Although many people love the idea of having boulders for shoulders, overworking these muscles can lead to problems. Remember, both the rotator cuff muscles and the deltoids will be worked during any upper body movement. The anterior deltoids work during pushing movements such as bench presses. The posterior deltoids work during pulling movements. The medial deltoids are worked in all exercises in which the arms are away from your body in the abducted position. The main role of the medial deltoids is to elevate your arm perpendicularly to your body (abduction). When trained properly, the deltoids can be both appealing and physically functional.

Shoulder Press

The king of shoulder exercises is certainly the shoulder press, also known as the military press. This exercise can be performed using a machine, barbell, or dumbbells. If you use a barbell or dumbbells, you can perform the exercise from either a sitting or standing position, although only advanced lifters should perform this exercise while standing. Shoulder presses can be performed by moving the weight in front or in back of the head, but I recommend moving the weight to the front of the head. Once you have good technique and range of motion, you may try lowering the weight behind your head. Let's start with a seated dumbbell shoulder press moving the weight in front of the head.

Sit on a weight bench, holding a dumbbell in each hand. Lift the dumbbells to your shoulders, palms out, elbows in line with your shoulders.

Starting position.

Push weight up from shoulders.

Push the weights up until your arms are fully extended. Pause momentarily at the top of the motion. Gently lock your elbows. Keep your torso tight and your chest and chin up during this exercise.

Return the weights to the starting position at your shoulders. Resist the momentum as the weights descend.

To bust out your boulders, use proper form. Do not compromise your lower back in order to use more weight. Do not use momentum or bounce the weight during the movement. Since this is an overhead exercise, it will strain the vertebrae and discs in your back while dispersing the load. Overtraining the shoulders is the most common symptom of using too much weight too quickly. It is better to underdo it than to overdo it.

Pause at the top.

Lower weight to starting position.

Barbell Shoulder Press

The barbell shoulder press can be performed while sitting on a weight bench or while standing, although the sitting position is recommended for beginners. Hold the bar, hands slightly more than shoulder-width apart, so that it touches the top of your chest. Push the bar overhead, fully extending your arms. Lean back only far enough to allow the bar to pass in front of your head. You also can start this exercise with your arms fully extended, lowering the weight to your chest as the first movement.

Barbell shoulder press.

Front raise.

Front Raise

The next three shoulder exercises isolate each of the three deltoid muscles. The front raise targets the anterior deltoid. Sit on a weight bench, arms at your sides, hands holding the dumbbells slightly to the front of your body. Your palms should be turned toward you. Raise the dumbbells straight out in front of you until your arms are about shoulder height. Lower the dumbbells back to the starting position. You also can perform this exercise with a barbell. Using an incline bench increases the range of motion

Lateral Raise

The lateral raise, also called the side raise, isolates the medial deltoid. You can perform this exercise standing (as shown) or sitting on a weight bench. Hold the dumbbells at your sides with your palms turned toward you. Raise your arms laterally until they are parallel with the ground, forming 90-degree angles at your armpits. Keep your elbows slightly bent. Lower the weights to the starting position.

Lateral raise.

Rear Deltoid Fly

The rear deltoid fly works the posterior deltoid and requires a little more patience. Lie face down on a weight bench. Drop your arms straight down and grab the dumbbells with your palms facing each other. Raise your arms to the sides and away from your body until they are parallel with the floor. Keep your elbows slightly bent. Pause momentarily at the top of the movement, then return the weights to the floor. Try to keep the weights suspended from the floor.

Rear deltoid fly.

Deltoids: Nature's Shoulder Pads

Big shoulders are a must if you are tired of wearing shoulder pads. Focusing on these hard-to-work muscles is the key to developing size. However, be careful not to overtrain. The most important concept to remember is that less is better than more. Since these muscles are used during almost every upper body exercise, often one to two sets of isolated shoulder work is plenty when mixed with other exercises. If you train your shoulders on their own, be sure to allow adequate rest between workouts.

Try to use dumbbells as much as possible. Dumbbells not only develop your ability to stabilize and balance the weight, strengthening the rotator cuff, but they also provide a greater range of motion.

Working the shoulder muscles can lead to back problems if you aren't cautious. Contract your abdominal muscles during the movement, and keep your head and chest up. Use lighter weights, and make your movements more defined. Do not use momentum to move the weights. Dropping your body to help lift the weight will only decrease the shoulder muscle involvement.

Since safety is of the utmost concern, using perfect form and minimizing lower back involvement are imperative. The most common error in weight training is to allow the body to bend and the lower back to round.

Gravity may be your worst enemy in performing overhead lifts. Be sure to clear your head; more than one lifter has gotten a good headache while performing shoulder presses. If you begin to feel yourself failing during the lift, lower the weight. Continuing after failure without a spotter can do serious damage to the shoulder capsule.

give it a go

DIG THESE DELTS

If you are prepared to work out more than three times a week, these shoulder routines will give you a good challenge. Routines 2 and 3 show a sample posterior and anterior combination routine for chest and back days.

WORK THE SHOULDERS

Routine 1	Routine 2	Routine 3
Shoulder press 3 × 10	Bench press 3 × 8	Seated row 3 × 10
Front raise 2 × 10	Shoulder press 2 × 8	Shoulder press 2 × 10
Rear deltoid fly 2 × 10	Rear deltoid fly 3 × 8	Front raise 3 × 10
Lateral raise 1 × 10		

Traps

A hallmark of bodybuilding success is to have traps that touch the ears, although your aspirations may not be as high. The trapezius muscle, or traps, is responsible for maintaining proper posture of the middle and upper back, the neck, and the shoulder blades.

The traps also help with the upper back exercises covered in chapter 3. Traps aid in pulling motions and help pull the shoulder blades together. When you shrug, you use the upper trapezius to lift your scapula. The traps rarely function alone, so isolating them is difficult. However, there are a few neat ways to target these muscles.

Shoulder Shrug

The shoulder shrug is definitely the most popular and easy to execute trapezius exercise. You can execute the exercise with either a barbell or dumbbells. The key to successful performance is tight form and relying on the traps to do the work. Avoid using your legs to initiate the movement.

To perform shoulder shrugs with a barbell, stand with feet about shoulder-width apart, knees gently locked. Hold the barbell at arm's length in front of you with your hands about shoulder-width apart, palms turned toward you. Lift your shoulders, squeezing your traps up toward your ears. Pause momentarily at the top, then lower the bar back to the starting position. You also can perform this exercise while holding the barbell behind your back.

Using a Barbell

Starting position, holding the barbell in front.

Squeeze the traps.

To perform shoulder shrugs with dumbbells, stand with feet about shoulder-width apart, knees gently locked. Hold one dumbbell in each hand at your sides with your palms turned toward you. Lift your shoulders, squeezing your traps. Pause momentarily at the top of the movement, then return the weights to the starting position.

Using Dumbbells

Starting position, holding the dumbbells to the side.

Squeeze the traps.

Upright Row

The main trap exercise besides the shoulder shrug is the upright row. The upright row primarily works the traps but gets a lot of help from the medial deltoids. Because the upright row puts pressure on the shoulder capsule, do not perform this exercise if you have shoulder problems. Stand with feet shoulder-width apart, knees gently locked. Hold the barbell in front, palms turned in. Pull the barbell straight up, shooting your elbows out to the sides. The bar should follow along your ribs until it hits the top of your chest. Pause momentarily at the top of the movement and shrug before slowly lowering the bar back to the starting point. Do not begin the motion by shrugging first or you will place the brunt of the load on the deltoids.

Remember, the traps work during many upper back exercises. The shoulder shrug and upright row are enough to give the traps a little extra work when combined with upper back exercises in a sound weight training program.

Upright row.

Including Psychological Muscle

As you execute shoulder shrugs, think about the movement you make when you say, "I don't know." The motion is exactly the same. If you lift heavy weights, use straps to hold onto the bar. Straps will decrease your development of grip strength, but using them will allow you to lift heavier weights.

Try verbalizing when you get to the top of the movement. Let out a big scream and nod your head back and forth like you are the boss. Although there is no physiological benefit to verbalizing, you may inspire the rest of the people in the gym to move out of your way. Of course, you also may be perceived as an idiot.

Avoid using your legs when you lift. Use of momentum will prevent proper development of the traps. Control the execution of the movement, pausing momentarily to allow the traps to develop, decrease the contribution of the deltoids, and prevent strain of the rotator cuff.

Many so-called experts will tell you to roll your shoulders forward and back at the top of the lift. This is not necessary and will not increase the emphasis on the traps. Worse yet, it may put the shoulder in a bad position. Although they are uncommon, shoulder dislocations have occurred when lifters tried to roll the shoulders.

Remember to think about the traps, say "I don't know," and work on isolating these muscles. Pull your traps to your ears and squeeze tight.

TRAINING THE TRAPS

Trapezius variations are not very complex, but keeping things simple is often more desirable. The mini programs will address the needs of your training routine and help maintain proper posture. Often trap work will be performed on the same day as shoulder work.

WORK THE TRAPS

Routine 1	Routine 2	Routine 3
Shoulder press 2 × 10	Shoulder shrug 3 × 8	Upright row 3 × 10
Shoulder shrug 2 × 10	Upright row 2 × 8	Shoulder shrug 3 × 10
Upright row 2 × 10	Rear deltoid fly 3 × 8	Rear deltoid fly 2 × 10
Rear deltoid fly 2 × 10		

Triceps

The triceps muscle group is responsible for extending the arm at the elbow. The triceps is involved in many throwing and pushing activities. As the name implies, the triceps muscle has three heads, all similar in function. Popular myth claims that these different heads can be developed individually with certain exercises, but most research indicates that genetics rather than training may be responsible for any differences. Bodybuilders want to develop this muscle to have a horseshoe-like appearance when contracted. The triceps muscle is an easy group to target, and any motion that extends the lower arm will work them well.

Triceps Pushdown

The triceps can be worked in several ways. One of the easiest, most effective ways is to use a cable machine to perform the triceps pushdown. This exercise may have its own station in the gym, or you can use the lat pulldown area. Select a bar attachment that is comfortable for your grip. Although many lifters think different types of bars hit the triceps differently, most research says otherwise.

Stand and grab the bar with palms turned out, hands at chest height. Your arms should be fully flexed with your elbows against your sides. Your hands should be approximately shoulder-width apart. (If you use an inverted-V bar, your hands will be slightly closer.)

Starting position.

Lock elbows at sides and lower the bar.

The motion is in a single plane. Lock your elbows at your sides and press the bar down until your arms are fully extended. Keep your elbows in during the entire movement. At the bottom position, squeeze your triceps.

Slowly return the bar to the starting position. To make the range of motion as large as possible, bring the bar all the way back up to chest height. Some lifters return the bar only to about waist height before beginning the next rep, but you want to use as large a range of motion as possible. Before you begin the next rep, your elbow angle should be as small as possible.

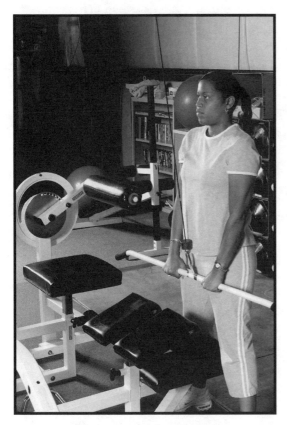

Squeeze triceps at bottom position.

Return bar to starting position.

Supine Triceps Extension

The supine triceps extension, also known as the skull crusher, nose breaker, or head caver, targets the triceps effectively when performed properly. Lie on your back on a weight bench. Grab the bar (a cambered bar is more comfortable to grip) and bring it to a position just behind your head. Your elbows should point straight forward and up. The angle at the armpit should be about 120 degrees. Your palms should be up. Fully extend your arms. When your arms are fully extended, the weight should be over your forehead, not over your eyes. Keeping the arms in proper position keeps the tension on the triceps.

Supine triceps extension.

Dip

The dip is definitely the king of triceps exercises. Dips also work the chest and front deltoids. To do dips, you need to have plenty of strength and balance. The great thing about doing dips is that you use your own body weight. If you can't complete a full set of dips, then do as many as you can. In time, you will be amazed at how easy they are. Hoist yourself onto the parallel bars with your body between them. Start with your arms fully extended by your sides. Bend your elbows, slowly lowering yourself between the bars until your elbows form a 90-degree angle. Pause momentarily, then return to the starting position by pushing down against the bars.

Dip on parallel bars.

Bench dip.

Bench Dip

If you have trouble performing dips on parallel bars, the modified bench dip is a good alternative. Begin with your feet on a flat bench and your legs fully extended. Your arms should be shoulder-width apart with your hands on the bench directly behind you, fingertips facing forward. This is a slightly awkward position, and you will feel a stretch across your chest. Bend your elbows, slowly lowering your body until your elbows form a 90-degree angle. Pause momentarily, then return to the starting position by pushing your arms downward.

Dumbbell Triceps Kickback

Another popular exercise is the dumb-bell triceps kickback. In this exercise, you work one arm at a time. Keep your elbow high during the movement. Stand with feet about shoulder-width apart, knees slightly bent. Lean forward and place your nonlifting hand on a knee for support. Maintain a flat back. Grasp the dumbbell firmly in your lifting hand. Point your elbow toward the ceiling. Extend your lifting arm back as far as comfortable. Full extension should feel slightly uncomfortable; if it doesn't, your elbow may not be high enough. Pause briefly at the top, then return to the starting position.

Dumbbell triceps kickback.

Overhead triceps kickback.

Overhead Triceps Kickback

A variation of the dumbbell triceps kickback is to perform the same movement overhead. You can either stand with feet shoulder-width apart or sit on a weight bench. Keep your back flat. Hold the dumbbell in one hand. Bring your lifting elbow up next to your ear. Point your elbow toward the ceiling. Fully extend your arm. The dumbbell will travel behind your head to the overhead position.

Tips to Tone Triceps

Proper execution is the key to success. During triceps exercises, the less you move your elbow back and forth, the more you emphasize the triceps. Maintaining proper posture is a must. To keep proper posture, contract your abs and keep your chest up. Many lifters note that the abs feel like they work during triceps exercises. This is a good thing, because it means that proper body posture is being used.

Use a thumb-lock grip. A loose grip will prevent overexertion, but you need to be able to hold onto the barbell or dumbbell. The most important tip, however, is to make sure that the plates are secured to the barbell or dumbbell. You will quickly learn why supine triceps extensions are called nose breakers if a plate falls off while you are performing one.

To get a true horseshoe-like appearance in your triceps, use the entire range of motion. That means using a smaller dumbbell and lighter weights. When you extend your arms, use a gentle lock at your elbows; do not snap them into a full lockout.

Although injuries are rare, olecranon bursitis (swelling in the elbow) may occur if your overdo it. If your elbow is sore, do not do triceps exercises. If you feel a slight pain during a particular exercise, try a different hand grip. It is not uncommon to find that some exercises bother the elbow, but others don't.

COMBINATIONS THAT TARGET THE TRICEPS

Since triceps extend the elbow and any pushing motion works the triceps, work on this group during the push day or chest day of your training program. Any triceps exercise will do—variety keeps working out enjoyable. The table shows some popular combinations. Routine 3 can be used during any push or chest day. Take a 60- to 90-second break between triceps exercises.

WORK THE TRICEPS

Routine 1	Routine 2	Routine 3
Bench press 2 × 10	Bench press 3 × 10	Dip 1 × 10
Pec fly* 2 × 8	Dip 2 × 10	Supine triceps extension 1 × 10
Supine triceps extension 2 × 8	Triceps pushdown 2 × 12	Triceps pushdown 1 × 10
Triceps pushdown 1 × 8	Pec fly* 2 × 12	Overhead triceps kickback 1 × 10

*The machine pec fly may be used instead of the dumbbell pec fly.

Biceps

The biceps are the most flexed and visible muscles of the body. In many cases, the biceps are the focal point of a lifter's routine. Interestingly, this two-headed muscle is not the only one that flexes the arm. Two other strong flexors, the brachialis and brachioradialis, work when you target this area. Contrary to popular belief, no single exercise can develop the biceps' specific shape. Hard work and some help from genetics are necessary.

Dumbbell Curl

The easiest biceps exercise to perform is also one of the best ways to target the biceps. The dumbbell curl can be performed sitting or standing, alternating arms or moving both together.

Stand with your arms fully extended down at your sides. Grab the dumbbells with your hands semipronated, your thumbs facing forward. Slowly begin to flex your arm.

The dumbbell should follow an arc as the angle at your elbow decreases. Your elbow should be fixed at your side during the entire movement. During the movement, twist the dumbbell so your palm faces forward to activate the biceps properly. This twisting motion is not required, but it does allow the dumbbell to pass your body with-

Starting position.

Raise dumbbell to shoulder.

out contact. If you keep your hands semipronated during the movement, you will focus more on the brachioradialis, giving the front of the lower arm more of a challenge.

Bring the dumbbell to your shoulder and squeeze your biceps tight for two counts. Slowly lower the dumbbell back to the starting position.

Since this is a popular muscle to train, there are many biceps exercises. Some of the more common ones include the isolated dumbbell curl, straight bar curl, cable curl, and preacher curl. In each of these exercises, the hand position can be altered to create even more variety.

Squeeze biceps at top of movement.

Lower weight to starting position.

Isolated Dumbbell Curl

In the isolated dumbbell curl, one arm is worked at a time. Sit on a weight bench. Press the back of your working arm against your inner thigh. Begin with the dumbbell in your hand, your arm fully extended. Slowly flex your arm, lifting the weight to your shoulder. Pause at the top of the movement and squeeze your biceps. Return the weight to the starting position. For variation, turn your palm inward as if you were holding a hammer and follow the same curling motion, keeping your lower arm in this position throughout the movement. This curl targets the brachioradialis slightly more and is known as the hammer curl.

Isolated dumbbell curl.

Straight Bar Curl

Probably the most common curl is the standing curl, also known as the straight bar curl. This exercise can be done with a standard straight bar-bell (straight bar curl) or a cambered bar (standing curl). Stand behind the barbell. Lock your hands around the bar, palms up, hands spread a little more than shoulder-width apart. Stand holding the barbell, arms fully extended. Slowly raise the barbell to your shoulders. The weight follows an arc until the arms are fully flexed. Lower the bar to the starting position under control; it will take about four seconds to lower it. Avoid low back injuries by making the biceps work harder—don't lean back. For variation, start with your hands spread wider on the bar, six inches or so from your body.

Straight bar curl.

Cable Curl

The cable curl can be done using a single handle fixed to a low pulley position on a machine. Grab the handle with both hands and pull it up to the extended-arm starting position. Force yourself to keep your elbows in at your sides. Slowly flex your arms, raising the handle to your shoulders. Squeeze your biceps at the top of the movement. Slowly return to the starting position. For variation, try the hammer curl position (see isolated dumbbell curl).

Cable curl.

Preacher curl.

Preacher Curl

Finally, the preacher curl makes a great isolated movement and can be performed using a preacher bench or with a machine. This exercise does a good job of isolating the arm by fixing it and preventing cheating by using other muscles. If you use a preacher bench, you can use either a cambered bar or a straight bar.

If you use a machine, make sure your elbows are lined up properly with the machine. (If you use the preacher bench, lean over the preacher bench, fixing your armpits tight to the bench.) Grab the handles on the machine, palms up, arms extended. Slowly flex your arms, bringing the handles to your shoulders. Pause at the top of the movement and squeeze your biceps. Slowly return to the starting position.

Building Better Biceps

A trick for standing exercises is to bend your legs slightly, taking pressure off your lower back, and stagger your feet to create more balance. As the weight gets farther from your body during the movement, you will need more force to overcome the weight's relative weight. You need good balance and control.

One of the biggest mistakes lifters make is to start the movement by launching the bar or dumbbell with momentum. Creating momentum at the waist causes the lifter to lean back, moving the tension from the biceps to other muscle groups. Lifters often cheat at biceps exercises when it gets most difficult, usually at the 90-degree angle. However, working through that sticking point will truly enhance overall improvement in the biceps. The desire to cheat by launching the weight with momentum is natural, but the best results will come if you force yourself to work harder when it gets harder.

Developing the biceps takes time and patience. Don't give up on them. Any pulling exercise will work these muscles. If you are having a difficult time developing these muscles, try isolating your arm muscles by inserting an arm-only day into your training program once a week. No single exercise can effectively target a specific area of the biceps, so your keys to success are performing a variety of exercises and using a full range of motion.

Another good tip is to get a spotter to assist you. Don't be afraid to get some help. Instead of using momentum and cheating through the tough areas, get a buddy to help you a little, and force your body to remain upright during the lift. To really work your biceps, try 10 reps with a heavy weight, forcing the last few reps.

give it a go

"AS SEEN ON TV" ARMS

I recommend working the biceps during pulling days, for example, when you plan upper back exercises. However, if you are really trying to focus on the arms, plan a separate day just for arm training. The table shows some classic routines. Routine 3 is for the TV arm day.

The TV arm day is named to describe the results of the workout. When routine 3 is performed for two or three giant sets (a set includes one set of all exercises for 10 reps), this workout will make your arms swell to a never-before-seen size, making them look fabulous on TV (at least, many athletes seem to think so).

WORK THE BICEPS

Routine 1	Routine 2	Routine 3*
Lat pulldown 3 × 10	Seated row 3 × 12	Supine triceps extension 1 × 10
Seated row 3 × 10	Straight bar curl 2 × 12	Straight bar curl 1 × 10
Straight bar curl 1 × 12	Preacher curl 2 × 12	Triceps pushdown 1 × 10
Dumbbell curl 1 × 12	Isolated dumbbell curl 1 × 12	Cable curl 1 × 10

*TV arm day

Forearms

Although back strength and leg strength are very important, if you can't hold onto something, it will be next to impossible to lift it, no matter how strong you are. The forearms contain many muscles that flex the wrist and fingers. Eating spinach has been shown to increase the size of the forearms in some cartoon characters, but most people need to perform gripping-type exercises to see improvements. The forearms get a lot of work during many pulling exercises if done without using lifting straps.

Wrist Curl

This easy exercise works both sides of the arm. Either dumbbells or a barbell can be used; however, the barbell's length makes it more difficult to manipulate.

Kneel next to a chair or weight bench with your forearms resting on the chair or bench and your wrists hanging over the edge. Grab the dumbbells with your palms facing up. You can work one arm at a time or both arms simultaneously.

Working the Flexors

Starting position.

Flexing the wrists.

Slowly raise and lower the dumbbells by flexing and releasing your wrists. Make each movement deliberate and go through the full range of motion. This movement will work the flexors, the major muscles on the inside of the arms.

To work the extensors on the back side of your arms, rest the insides of your forearms on the chair or bench. Grab the dumbbells with your palms facing down. Slowly raise and lower the dumbbells by flexing and releasing your wrists.

Working the Extensors

Starting position.

Flexing the wrists.

The variety of exercises that work this muscle group is rather meager. One variation that works your grip is hanging wrist work. Grab very large dumbbells and hold them at your sides for as long as you can.

Another variation is to use a slightly lighter dumbbell and roll it to the ends of your fingers and back up. In other words, open your hand until the weight reaches the ends of your fingers, then curl your fingers and roll the dumbbell back into your palm. Perform this exercise with extreme caution; if you drop the weight, your toes may never forgive you.

A third variation is to buy a set of grippers. Hold the grippers in your hands and squeeze them tight.

Forearm Exercise Variations

Hanging wrist work.

Grippers.

Get a Grip!

The heavier the weight you use and the slower you perform the movement, the greater the training effect will be. Do not neglect this area in your training, especially if you play tennis, golf, baseball, softball, or any other sport that requires you to hold a hitting implement.

Using dumbbells with spinning plates allows the weight to move properly, but if you don't have dumbbells with spinning plates, don't worry. For the most part, if the dumbbell plates are secure, then wrist curls are safe. It is difficult to do any major damage unless you really overwork your wrists. The first few times you do these exercises, you may get sore, but in time the soreness will go away and your grip strength will improve dramatically.

WINNING WRIST WORK

As stand-alone exercises, wrist curls and gripping exercises can be done anytime, anywhere. Typically, they are incorporated into pulling or back and biceps workouts. Gripping muscles also are worked heavily during biceps activity. The table shows the recommended sequence when incorporating wrist training with a back and biceps workout or doing wrist exercises on their own.

WORK THE WRISTS

Routine 1	Routine 2
Lat pulldown 2 × 10	Wrist curl, flexors and extensors 2 × 10 each
Seated row 2 × 10	Hanging wrist work 2 × time
Biceps curl (any variation) 3 × 10	Gripper 2 × 10 each hand
Wrist curl, flexors and extensors 2 × 10 each	

Abs

Even many nonlifters dream of having a well-toned six-pack, a washboard stomach that is the envy of everyone on the beach. Before we move into training your abs, though, we need to shatter a few myths. First, the idea of spot reduction—that you can lose weight in one specific area of the body—is a fallacy. Second, you don't need fancy, expensive machines to work your abs. Finally, and perhaps the hardest to accept, is that many people who train hard will never see their toned abs. Most people are not lean enough to see the six-pack. The good news is that the visual impact of the abs is rather meaningless. Strong abdominals create stability at your core, reduce your risk of developing back problems, improve posture, and increase sport performance. More good news is that these so-called hard-to-develop muscles are not hard to develop at all.

We will focus on three major abdominal muscles. The main abdominal muscle that runs down the middle of your body is the rectus abdominus. The obliques on the sides of your body allow you to twist. The transverse abdominus provide support. All ab muscles work during every abdominal exercise. Twisting only slightly increases the effort from the obliques. The main role of the abdominal muscles is trunk flexion (allows you to sit up) and pelvic stabilization (allows you to dance without falling over).

Curl-Up

For many years, this exercise was called a sit-up, but it has been modified to prevent neck and low back injuries. Often this exercise is called a crunch. Research shows that curl-ups activate all abdominal muscles as much as any other exercise. In fact, curl-ups cause greater activation of the abs than most ab machines advertised on TV.

Lie on your back with your knees bent and together or slightly apart, your feet flat on the ground about shoulder-width apart. You can perform this exercise with your hands by your sides. If you place your hands behind your head, be careful; the extra strain may damage the neck vertebrae. Do not pull on your neck when you curl up.

Starting position.

Curl your trunk up to the point at which the middle of your back comes off the floor, but keep your lower back touching the floor.

Perform the movement slowly. Jerky movements will bypass the abdominal muscles in favor of the much stronger hip flexors. Squeeze at the top position for two counts, then slowly return to the starting position.

Once you have progressed to the point where you can perform many repetitions without losing proper form, you can increase the intensity of the curl-up by extending your arms to your sides.

Lift the middle back off the floor.

Twisting Curl-Up

The most popular variation is a twisting curl-up, which activates the obliques a little more. Lie on your back, knees bent. Put your hands over your ears and flare your elbows out to your sides. Curl up, but twist at the waist as you near the top of the movement, moving one elbow toward the opposite knee. Remember, slow, precise movement is the key. If you move too quickly, you won't work the abs.

Twisting curl-up.

Side Bend

The side bend also concentrates more on the obliques. Stand with your feet shoulder-width apart, knees slightly bent. With a dumbbell in each hand, arms straight at your sides, slowly lean side to side, accentuating the range of motion. Both sets of obliques will work in each direction as you lower and raise. If you prefer, you can work one side at a time. Hold one dumbbell and place the other hand behind your head for optimal balance.

Side bend.

Pelvic Raise

The pelvic raise is safe and effective at targeting the lower abs, although you should not perform this exercise if you have a sore back. Lie on your back. Raise your legs, crossing your ankles and bending your knees slightly. The soles of your feet should point toward the ceiling. Contract your abs, raising your buttocks off the ground. Hold at the top of the movement. Don't expect a lot of movement; the actual amount may be only a few inches. Do not try to increase the movement by thrusting your hips into the air.

Pelvic raise.

Slow Down to Tone Up

To train your abs better than ever, remember this one piece of advice: slow down the movement. During curl-ups, imagine a chain is attached to your rib cage, and someone at the other end is cranking you up one link at a time. Allow yourself to be slowly pulled up, completely contracting your abs one segment at a time. By slowing down the movement, you force the abs to work harder by removing the momentum generated by other muscles.

Do not work the abs when your back is sore. Keep your torso erect, and don't tuck your chin into your chest. To develop abdominal endurance, perform more reps. If strength is your goal, increase the resistance by altering your arm position or adding weight. Having a gym buddy press against you while you try to do curls may be a good challenge. Advanced lifters can use medicine balls for an additional abdominal challenge.

Take your time and be patient. Being able to see your six-pack may take much longer than their actual development.

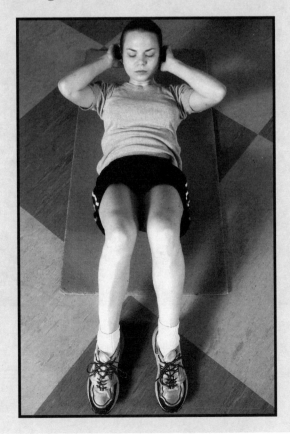

ABSOLUTE ABS

Abs, like any other muscle, need rest. Contrary to popular belief, abs should not be worked every day, and you do not have to perform hundreds of reps. Abs can be worked on their own. When performing 15 reps becomes easy, add resistance by holding a weight plate over your face or chest. Ab work can be added to any program or performed alone. Most people save ab exercises until the end of the workout, but whatever you do, don't neglect them. It may be better to perform them on their own or between other exercises.

WORK THE ABS

Routine 1	Routine 2	Routine 3
Curl-up 2 $\times$ 12	Perform in circuit for two sets of each exercise	Side bend 3 $\times$ 12 each side
Twisting curl-up 1 $\times$ 15 each side	Curl-up 1 $\times$ 15	Curl-up 3 $\times$ 12
Pelvic raise 1 $\times$ 15	Twisting curl-up 1 $\times$ 15 each side	
	Pelvic raise 1 $\times$ 15	

Lower Back

The lower back is key to all movement. Soreness and injury in this area can have a profound effect on training, sport performance, and everyday life. Nearly 80 percent of all people will experience back problems at some time. Although most injuries are just strains, major problems can also occur. Strains can be caused by improper lifting techniques or because of weak low back muscles and abs. Many injuries can be prevented by strengthening these muscles.

The back is a complex web of ligaments and muscles that perform finite to general movements. Several layers of muscles run the length of the back, attaching at different vertebrae along the way. The main function of the lower back is trunk extension and stabilization. Twisting is also possible, which is one of the main ways people injure their backs. Light back work should be incorporated into all programs.

Back Extension

Back extensions, also called hyperextensions or hypers, work the lower back from a bent-over position. Straightening the body is back extension. A specially designed bench or machine can be used to increase resistance.

Sit down on the bench with your arms crossed over your chest and your upper back against the pad. Knees should be slightly flexed, with legs stable.

Starting position.

Slowly push back against the pad to straighten your torso. Hold at the extended straight position for two counts. Slowly return to the starting position.

Hold the extended position.

Most exercises for the lower back require a high degree of skill. The straight-leg deadlift requires good foundational strength and is recommended only for more advanced lifters. It demands extremely good technique. This lift works the hamstrings, lower back, and glutes. To take some pressure off the lower back, slightly bend your knees.

The key is to keep the bar as close to your body as possible. If the bar travels too far away from your body or your form deteriorates, you may do considerable damage to your back.

Straight-Leg Deadlift

Stand with your feet about shoulder-width apart, perpendicular to the barbell, the bar resting on the floor across your shins. Bend at your waist, keeping your legs almost straight with about 10 degrees of knee flexion. Grasp the bar just wider than shoulder-width with the palms turned toward you. Keep your arms fully extended during the entire movement. Stick your chest out and pull up on the bar to reduce any slack in your legs or arms. Slowly pull the bar up, keeping your arms locked and your back flat. Pull the bar along your legs until it is at waist height with your arms fully extended. Keep the bar as close to your body as possible during the entire lift. Slowly lower the barbell; do not drop it. Proper control is essential. The torso should remain tight during the entire lift. Do not do this exercise if your back is sore.

For a body weight variation, use the same movement but without the barbell. Use only the weight of your upper torso for resistance.

Straight-leg deadlift.

Don't Break Your Back

Safety is the biggest concern for all back exercises. Perform all back exercises slowly. During straight-leg deadlifts, keep the bar close to your body. The farther the bar is from your body, the more tension will be placed on the lumbar discs and the harder you will have to work to control the weight. When you finish a set, you may want to stretch your lower back and take a slightly longer rest period. For a quick stretch, grab hold of a machine or post, extend your arms, and round your upper back by leaning away from the pole.

As with all exercises, proper technique is a must. Contract the abs to keep your torso erect; this will help stabilize your entire body. Do not use a weight belt when performing back exercises unless a physician tells you to do so. Back exercises strengthen your core; the belt will reduce this effect. Respect your lower back; do not work your back if it is sore. If the soreness persists for more than a day or two, see a physician.

STRENGTHEN YOUR BACK

The lower back is usually exercised on leg days and at the very end of the routine, if at all. Never perform lower back exercises the day before leg work; you won't have enough time to recover between workouts. Use a relatively light weight for 10 to 12 repetitions of two to three sets, depending on how your back feels.

Since it is unlikely you would work your back alone (nor is this recommended), the routines in the table suggest possible set-rep scenarios only. Routine 1 can be used to develop strength, routine 2 is for strength and endurance, and routine 3 is for endurance. Use lighter weights for routine 3.

WORK THE BACK

Routine 1	Routine 2	Routine 3
Straight-leg deadlift 2 × 10	Straight-leg deadlift 1 × 12	Straight-leg deadlift 2 × 15
Back extension 2 × 10	Straight-leg deadlift 1 × 8	Back extension 2 × 15
	Back extension 2 × 12	

Glutes and Hips

Everyone wants to have a tighter backside. The gluteus maximus, gluteus medius, and gluteus minimus, collectively referred to as the glutes, make up the major muscles of the buttocks. These muscles help pull the leg back. The gluteus medius, with the help of a few other muscles such as the tensor fasciae latae and the sartorius on the outer thigh, move the leg to the side. Several other muscles, including the gracilis and adductor magnus of the inner thigh, bring the leg back in. The psoas major and iliacus muscles at the front of the hip help bring the knee to the chest. The entire group of muscles acts on the hip for both movement and stabilization.

Infomercials promoting home machines have led many to believe that these muscles can be individually targeted. Sorry to burst that bubble, but spot reduction is a fallacy. Even most health club butt blaster machines work the quadriceps muscles of the leg first, rather than the pelvic muscles. Only isolated hip extension, adduction, and abduction can truly target the glutes. Since the gluteus maximus is responsible for hip extension, one grand exercise can work the whole area.

Leg Press

Before the creation of the leg press, the squat—heralded as the king of all exercises—was a mainstay for all strength and mass building programs. However, since the squat is not easy to learn, we'll begin with the leg press. We'll discuss the squat in the next chapter as a quadriceps exercise, although it requires significant contribution from the glutes. Allow this chapter to serve as a progression before attempting the much more difficult squat.

There are several different kinds of leg presses, but all will work the muscles adequately. The key is to select a machine that is comfortable and takes pressure off your back. Leg presses work just about every muscle in the lower body, although the glutes and adductors will work the most.

Foot position is vital for proper alignment during the lift and for emphasizing specific muscles. Begin with your feet higher up on the footpads, toes pointing out slightly. Pointing the toes out helps the body follow its normal path and prevents the knees from bending in.

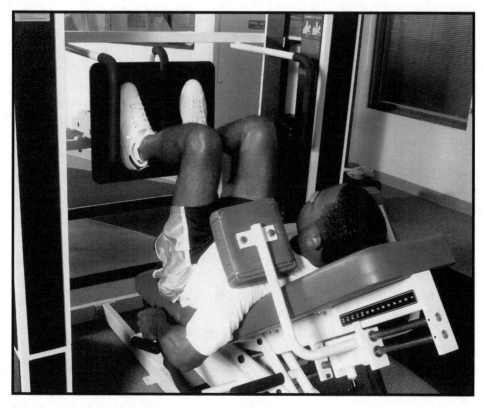

Starting position, knees bent.

The farther apart your legs are, the more the adductors will have to work during the movement.

Depending on the machine, the movement may begin with your knees at your chest or your legs fully extended. In either case, when the legs are flexed, the thighs should be parallel with the footpads. During the extension phase, you can gently lock your knees; do not snap your knees into place.

Slowly and steadily extend your legs. Do not bounce at the bottom. Do not let your knees track past your toes. The lower leg should be perpendicular to the footpad. Contract your abs and lower back to keep your body stable. Maintain an erect posture. Do not let your lower back round, and keep your head up and chest out.

Pause momentarily at the bottom of the movement to prevent momentum from rushing the flexion stage. The flexion stage may be slightly faster, but keep it under control. Slowly bend your knees, bringing them close to your chest.

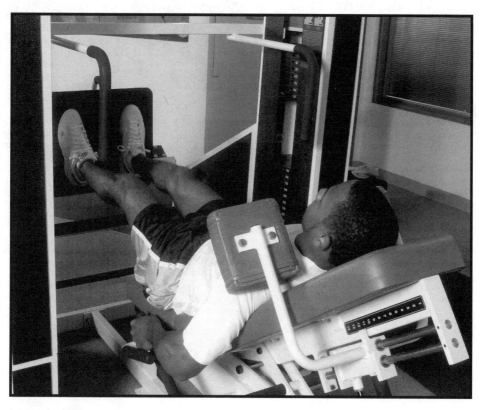

Leg extension.

Using a hip extensor machine is a great way to isolate the glutes. A low pulley attached to a multistation cable machine can be used for a variety of exercises working the glutes and hips, including low-cable kickbacks, side-cable lifts, adductor cable lifts, and hip flexor cable lifts. Collectively, these four low-pulley exercises are referred to as the four-way hip.

Hip Extension

The hip extensor machine can be adjusted for a larger range of motion. The larger the range of motion, the more the glutes are involved. Begin with one leg on the ground for support, the other leg attached to the weight cord. Pull the working leg back and away from the body. Keep the torso erect during the movement, and do not thrust the leg back violently. Pause momentarily at the top of the movement before returning the working leg to the starting position.

Hip extension.

Low-Cable Kickback

Add a low pulley strap to a multistation cable machine so that the pulley is on the floor. A simple belt will do if no special strap is available. Stand facing the weight stack. Hook the pulley around the ankle of your working leg. Use the other leg for support. Pull the strapped leg back against the resistance. Maintain proper posture throughout the lift. The greater the range of motion, the more the glutes will be worked.

Low-cable kickback.

Side-Cable Lift

You can also use the low pulley to target the outer thigh, working the adductors, abductors, and hip flexors. Stand next to the weight stack and hook the pulley around the ankle of your outside leg. Pull your leg to the side away from your body. Slowly return to the starting position, resisting the weight as you lower your leg.

Side-cable lift.

Adductor Cable Lift

The low pulley can also be used to work the adductors of the inner thigh. Stand beside the weight stack. Hook the pulley around the ankle of your inner leg. Pull your leg across your body, away from the weight stack. Slowly return to the starting position, resisting the pull of the weight.

Adductor cable lift.

Hip Flexor Cable Lift

With the low pulley on the cable machine, turn away from the weight stack. Hook the low pulley around the ankle of your working leg. Kick your working leg straight out in front, working the hip flexors. Slowly return to the starting position.

Hip flexor cable lift.

Getting Great Legs

Foot placement during leg presses determines which muscles will be worked the most. If your feet are close together, generally you will work the outside of your thighs more. If your feet are wide apart, you will emphasize the inner thighs, hamstrings, and glutes more. Although the difference may be small, changing your foot position will help improve overall hip stability and add variety.

During leg presses, try to push yourself away from the weight rather than pushing the weight away from you. Your focus shifts from fear of being crushed by the weight to dominance over the weight.

Make sure the machine is adjusted properly for you. If it doesn't feel right, then it probably isn't. Have someone familiar with the machine adjust it for you.

The key to tight buns is to work deep into the muscle and increase the range of motion. If leg presses are too hard on your knees, try the isolated, single-leg movements. Don't jerk the weight; use smooth, regular contractions. Work the hip in all four directions, rather than focusing on having a tight backside or thigh.

Strengthening the entire hip capsule will improve all aspects of balance and strength. Toning these muscles will not only give your hips and backside a nice shape, but it will help increase speed and strength for lower body activities. Having strong muscles around the hip also decreases the potential for hip fractures later in life.

You will have to endure some pretty tough workouts to see good definition in these muscles. Trembling legs are just a minor symptom of hard work. Make it through these initially difficult workouts and your training volume will improve, and so will your results. However, be smart and listen to your body. If your back is sore, discontinue these exercises.

Patience is a virtue. You didn't get out of shape in a day, and you won't get back into shape in a day. Think of this area as a long-term project.

COMBO LEG ROUTINES

For a complete hip and lower body workout, simply do a few sets of leg presses plus the four-way hip. However, several other combinations include the quadriceps and hamstrings. The table shows several good routines. Routine 1 is a good general program for overall lower body development. Routine 2 works a few extra muscles and may be a good way to work everything if you are short on time.

WORK THE GLUTES AND HIPS

Routine 1	Routine 2
Leg press 4 × 10; vary foot position each set	Leg press 2 × 10
Four-way hip 1 × 10 in each direction; rest after each direction	Straight-leg deadlift 2 × 10
Repeat for a second circuit	Four-way hip 1 × 10 each direction

Quads

Muscle balance doesn't only refer to balance front to back. It also refers to balance top to bottom. Some lifters focus so much on upper body development that they neglect their chopstick-like legs. The quadriceps (or quads) in the upper leg are made up of four muscles. The vastus lateralis, vastus medialis, and vastus intermedius all help extend the lower leg at the knee. The rectus femoris crosses two joints: the hip, where it helps in hip flexion, and the knee, where it helps extend the lower leg. Although the quads don't originate at the same point, they all come together at the kneecap.

There is much speculation about whether or not each individual quad can be isolated or stressed to a greater extent. To date, the mostly anecdotal evidence has shown mixed results. Concern yourself with properly executing the lift rather than trying to isolate a particular head.

Squat

Squats are like leg presses, only more demanding. The squat, the king of all lifts, works the quads hard. Before attempting squats, you need a proper base strength level. Once you have achieved this level, you will start with light weights. Squats using a barbell should not be attempted by beginners. Those with poor strength or flexibility should practice squats without weights before progressing to weights. Beginners can learn the correct technique by using no weights and squatting down to a chair or box. Too many career-ending back injuries have resulted from improper execution of this lift. For experienced lifters, after proper progression and regular training, squats can produce fabulous results.

Hold a barbell across your traps and shoulders using a thumb-lock grip. Keep your head up, chin pointing forward, and chest out during the entire movement. There will be a slight arch in your lower back. Place your feet wider than shoulder-width apart with your toes pointing out slightly.

Starting position.

Begin descent by pushing hips back.

Inhale deeply and contract your abs and back muscles to stabilize your body. Begin to lower your body by thrusting your hips back. A common mistake is to begin the movement by bending your knees, which can easily pull you out of position.

Continue to lower your body by moving your hips back and bending at your knees and waist. Lower yourself until your thighs are parallel to the floor. Keep your body tight and upright, and don't let your knees track past your toes.

Pause briefly at the bottom of the movement. To return to the starting position, exhale and powerfully thrust your hips under your body. Maintain proper back and neck posture during the entire movement. Finish the rep by locking your knees, as long as you control it. Do not pop into a lockout.

Lower until thighs are parallel to the floor.

Return to starting position.

Leg extensions are a good choice if you have access to a leg extension machine. If you don't, a lower body exercise that is gaining popularity is the lunge. Lunges are often used by athletes and weekend warriors looking to gain balance and strength. Stationary lunges will tone the legs as well as train stability and balance. The more advanced option, walking lunges, should not be performed until you have mastered stationary lunges.

Leg Extension

A leg workout is not complete without a few hard-fought reps on the leg extension machine. A leg extension machine can work each leg individually or both legs together, although it seems to be more chal-

lenging and beneficial to work both legs together. Adjust the machine's seat so that your knees are lined up directly with the machine arm's axis of rotation and your shins rest against the pad (legs start at about 90 degrees). Note your settings so you can use them later. If the machine has a belt, use it; you will need it when you work hard. Push against the pad until your legs are fully extended and are parallel to the ground. Either gently lock your knees or do not lock them at all. Keep the tension on your thighs the entire time. Do not throw the weight up; your body should remain in the machine.

Leg extension.

Lunge

For the stationary lunge, stand upright with your arms at your sides, one dumbbell in each hand. (Instead of dumbbells, you can use a barbell. Place the barbell across your traps and shoulders, using a thumb-lock grip.) Step forward a comfortable distance, about three feet. Keep your legs shoulder-width apart to help you balance the weight. Bend the forward knee until the thigh is parallel to the floor and the rear knee just skims the ground. The lead knee should not track over the toes. Pause briefly at the bottom. Push back on the lead foot to return to the starting position. This exercise may look easy, but don't let it fool you.

Lunge.

Walking Lunge

The walking lunge has the same starting position as the stationary lunge. Stand upright, arms at your sides, a dumbbell in each hand or a barbell across your shoulders. Step forward a comfortable distance, about three feet, keeping your legs shoulder-width apart. Bend the forward knee until the thigh is parallel to the floor and the rear knee just skims the ground. The lead knee should not track over the toes. Pause briefly at the bottom. Lean slightly forward to generate forward momentum for the next rep. Bring the back leg forward a comfortable step and bend the knee until the thigh is parallel to the floor. Continue for several steps.

Walking Lunge

Step forward and lunge.

Bring back leg forward and lunge with the other leg.

Tips for Quad Training

Two main tips: first, do not use a belt, wrap, or special device to help you lift; second, when you use a barbell, make sure the bar travels vertically up and down with little or no horizontal movement (except for walking lunges). Horizontal movement in either direction indicates flaws in technique. Using a belt cheats the abdominal and low back muscles out of their responsibility to protect and serve.

When you are starting out, don't be afraid to use just your body weight to learn correct technique before moving on to weights. Don't feel that you have to lift huge weights to reap the benefits of weight training. More important than using heavy weights is controlling the weight and using proper technique. Make sure you have established good balance and technique before lifting with heavy weights.

give it a go

TONE THE THIGHS

The table shows a few good programs that work the quads. Remember, work hard, play later.

WORK THE QUADS

Routine 1	Routine 2	Routine 3
Leg press 3 × 10	Leg press 2 × 12	Lunge 3 × 15
Leg extension 2 × 10	Walking lunge 2 × 12	Four-way hip 2 × 15 each direction
Four-way hip 1 × 10 each direction	Leg extension 2 × 8	Leg extension 2 × 15
	Leg curl 2 × 8	

13

CHAPTER

Hamstrings

The hamstrings, the muscles that run up the back of the upper leg, are crucial for support. They function opposite to the quadriceps. The three hamstring muscles cross both the hip and knee joints, making them responsible for both bending the knee and pulling the leg back. The hammys, or hams, are often neglected and undertrained and, as a result, are the most commonly pulled or strained muscle in the body. Proper development of the hamstrings will balance the body and reduce strain on the lower back. Lower back problems are often associated with weak and inflexible hamstrings.

Lying Leg Curl

The most popular exercise for hamstrings is definitely the lying leg curl. If possible, use a machine that allows for a slight bend in the hips. This decreases the likelihood of cheating and improves the isolation of the hamstrings. You can work each leg individually, but like the leg extension, this exercise is more beneficial if you work both legs at the same time.

Lie face down with your legs fully extended in the machine. The pad should rest just beneath your calf muscles.

Starting position.

The position of your knees with respect to the machine arm's axis of rotation is extremely important. Line up your knees with the dot on the cam of the machine. This ensures proper distribution of resistance from the machine.

With constant, even force, lift your heels to your buttocks and squeeze your hamstrings and glutes at the top position. Hold for two counts, then release. Lower the weight back to the starting position under control.

Squeeze at the top position.

The only way to truly isolate the hams is to use resistance against the motion of flexing the knee. Many lower body exercises activate the hams during the movement. For example, the straight-leg deadlift (see chapter 10) is often considered the next-best hamstring exercise to the lying leg curl. The seated leg curl and single-leg curl do a good job, too.

Seated Leg Curl

Begin with your legs straight out in front. The pad should rest against the Achilles tendons beneath your calf muscles. Pull your legs back toward your buttocks as far as you can and hold. Return to the starting position under control.

Seated leg curl.

Single-Leg Curl

If you like a challenge, try a standing single-leg curl. This exercise complements the four-way hip described in chapter 11. Add a low pulley strap to a multistation cable machine so that the pulley is on the floor. Stand facing the weight stack. Hook the pulley around the ankle of your working leg. Use the other leg for support. Bend the knee of the working leg, bringing your heel to your buttocks. Maintain proper posture and balance. If necessary, hold onto something stable to keep your balance.

Single-leg curl.

Focus on the Hams

The hamstrings perform two different actions: flexing the knee and extending the hip. Therefore, the hamstrings are targeted during any lift that flexes the knee or extends the hip. The hams are used when you squat, lunge, or perform straight-leg deadlifts or any other exercise that extends the hip. However, do not assume that your hams get enough work from other exercises. The lying leg curl is the best at isolating the hamstrings and preventing strains.

It is okay to squeeze your buttocks and pull your hips slightly off the bench when doing leg curls. The most important thing to remember is to use as large a range of motion as possible and squeeze tightly at the contracted position. If you want a real challenge, point your toes. This little modification eliminates the help of the calf muscles and makes the hamstrings work harder.

In your quest for muscle balance, don't forget to work the hammys. Isolate them in order to train them properly. Control your movements, and squeeze at the top of the movement. Don't rush.

TRAINING THE HAMSTRINGS

Full range of motion is the key to great-looking hams. Although the best way to isolate the hams is to do leg curls, exercise combinations will certainly work them well.

WORK THE HAMSTRINGS

Routine 1	Routine 2	Routine 3
Lying leg curl 2 × 12	Straight-leg deadlift 2 × 12	Lying leg curl 1 × 10
Seated leg curl 2 × 12	Seated leg curl 1 × 10 each leg	Seated leg curl 1 × 10
	Single-leg curl 1 × 10 each leg	Single-leg curl 1 × 15 each leg
		Complete minicircuit twice

Calves

The muscles on the back of the lower leg are known collectively as the calves. Advanced lifters who have bulked up these muscles call them cows. Two major calf muscles, the gastrocnemius and the soleus, and a host of other muscles help plantar flex the foot. The gastrocnemius (the larger muscle) can develop the heart-shaped appearance so highly desired by bodybuilders and is involved in foot and knee actions. The soleus lies deeper under the gastrocnemius. Both muscles can press the foot down strongly and are very important in jumping.

Do not forget the muscles on the front of the lower legs. Although many lifters hardly work them, these muscles are extremely important. Without them, you would not be able to flex your foot upward. These are the muscles that prevent you from tripping over your own feet. The main dorsiflexor is the anterior tibialis.

Heel Raise

This exercise is often inaccurately called the calf raise or toe raise. Both names refer to raising the wrong body part. To attack the calves properly, you need to raise your heel off the floor while pivoting on the balls of your feet. The exercise can be done on a machine or on a step. If you use the step, your own body weight probably will be sufficient resistance, but if you want to increase the intensity, pick up a couple of heavy dumbbells and hold them at your sides.

Stand on your tiptoes on the edge of the step or machine. The balls of your feet should be secure on the surface, with your heels hanging off the edge.

Starting position.

Raise heels.

Drive your toes into the ground as if stepping hard on a gas pedal. Your heels will move up. Pivot on the balls of your feet. Keep pressing your toes until your feet are fully extended. Keep your legs straight during the entire movement; since the gastrocnemius muscle crosses two joints, if the knees bend, the emphasis shifts to the soleus. Hold at the top before slowly returning to the starting position.

Hold at top of movement.

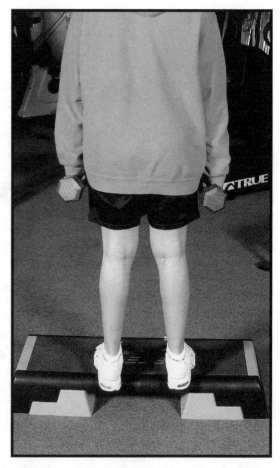

Return to starting position.

Single-Leg Heel Raise

An excellent variation of the heel raise is the single-leg heel raise. This exercise is similar to the heel raise except, to add more resistance, all the weight is on one foot. Stand on the edge of the machine or step with your heels hanging over the edge, as in the heel raise. Cross your nonworking leg behind your working leg. Press your toes to lift up your heel.

Single-leg heel raise.

Seated Calf

The seated calf targets the soleus by removing some of the powerful pulling action of the gastrocnemius. The range of motion for the seated calf is much shorter than for the standing heel raise, although the movement is similar. Sit in the seat of the machine with your knees bent, the resistance on your thighs rather than your shoulders. Place your feet on the foot bar with your heels hanging over the edge. Press your toes into the foot bar to lift your heels.

Seated calf.

Toe Pull

The toe pull strengthens the front of the lower leg. As its name implies, the motion of the exercise is to pull your toes toward your leg. A few gyms have a toe pull machine, but you can perform toe pulls without a machine by using a partner or a tube. Sit comfortably on a bench with your legs stretched out, your heels hanging over the edge of the bench. (If you do not have a bench, you can sit on the floor.) Point your toes as much as you can and have your partner grab your toes. Your partner will create the resistance. Flex your feet, pulling against the resistance created by your partner. Do not pull your legs back. The motion moves around the ankle joint. To use a tube, affix one end to an immovable object and the other around your toes.

Toe pull.

Developing Heart-Shaped Calves

The key to success in developing your calves is to realize that they work like any other muscle. For some reason, many lifters assume they need to perform hundreds of reps to achieve the desired look. The largest attributing factor to shape is genetics. Since these muscles are part of an efficient lever system, they can lift considerably more weight. Use heavier weight, but perform the same number of reps as you would for any other body part. Use the full range of motion, and perform each rep under control.

Anecdotal evidence suggests foot position variations may target the inner and outer portions of the gastrocnemius more effectively. Currently, these theories have not been proven conclusively. Feel free, however, to try pointing your toes in to work the outer head or pointing your toes out to work the inner head.

Calf muscles are easily strained. Before training your calves, warm them up and stretch them out. If they feel tight, do not train them. If you plan to perform long-duration aerobic activity such as running later that day or on the following day, work the calves lightly or not at all.

Work the muscle in a smooth action from start to finish. Do not jerk your heels upward. That is a no-no. Muscles work best when they are continually stressed through the entire range of motion. Don't sweat it. Your calves will tone; it may just take some time.

give it a go

TONING THE CALVES

You can work the calves in two ways: with legs extended or legs flexed. How you choose to get to that position is up to you. As long as you can create enough resistance, it is recommended to work the calves in both ways during each workout. If you are short on time, use one way for one workout, then the other way for the next workout, alternating every other workout.

Generally, size is the goal. For hypertrophy, go for 12 reps with no more than 90 seconds of rest between sets (60 seconds is preferred). If you can, perform another set, totaling three sets in all.

WORK THE CALVES

Routine 1	Routine 2	Routine 3
Heel raise 2 × 12	Seated calf 2 × 12	Heel raise 1 × 12
Toe pull 2 × 12	Toe pull 2 × 12	Seated calf 1 × 12
		Toe pull 2 × 12

Developing Your Program

Now that you know the basic principles of weight lifting and how to perform the exercises, it's time to develop your own program.

The concept of the perfect rep is probably the most important idea to take into the weight room. Every rep needs to be perfect. To adopt the perfect rep philosophy, tell yourself that no matter what speed the weight moves at and no matter what method you are using to train, your reps will be perfect—no cheating, no momentum, only perfect reps count. Think quality, not quantity.

A perfect rep has a two-second concentric phase followed by a three- to four-second eccentric phase. Perfect your form before adding more weight. The idea of the perfect rep agrees with the general principle of progression.

You can choose from several hundred different exercises with various modifications. With each exercise, you can use a machine, free weight, dumbbell, resistance band, or other form of resistance. In addition, each machine may vary in speed or leverage based on its cam or computer system. Each form of resistance has its advantages and disadvantages (see the table). Whichever mode you choose, make sure the exercise is specific to what you are trying to achieve and each rep is as perfect as possible.

COMPARING DIFFERENT TYPES OF RESISTANCE

Method of resistance	Pros	Cons
Free weights	Develop balance; work stabilizer muscles; challenging for most lifters	May require a partner; may require skill or technique that takes a long time to learn; do not isolate muscles
Isolateral machines	Allow for weaker arm or leg to develop individually and catch up to stronger arm or leg; excellent for rehab after an injury; isolate muscle; lifter can work out alone	Do not allow for development of stabilizer muscles
Combined machines	Excellent for rehab after an injury; isolate muscle; lifter can work out alone	Do not allow for development of stabilizer muscles; do not present enough challenge for some lifters
Dumbbells	No gym required—lifter can train alone at home; develop balance; work stabilizer muscles; challenging for most lifters; allow for weaker arm or leg to develop individually and catch up to stronger arm or leg; excellent for rehab after an injury; isolate muscle	Require skill; sometimes evenly balancing the weight overcomes primary emphasis of exercise
Resistance bands	Excellent for rehab; lifter can train alone at home	Make it hard to measure strength; bands may not create enough resistance; bands weaken and change strength curve over stretch (start out easier, get tougher); some lifters like to see the weight
Isokinetic machines	Cause muscles to produce maximal force throughout the entire range of motion at a specific controlled velocity	Very expensive and highly impractical for a complete training program

Types of Training Programs

Each training method has different set, rep, and resistance parameters. If you are following the overload principle, you will notice that the resistance becomes difficult by the last one or two reps of each set. No matter how many reps are required, the resistance should be challenging once you are familiar with the exercise. If you use weights that are too light, it will take longer to see results. If you use weights that are too heavy, you risk burnout, overtraining, and injury.

Training for Muscular Endurance

To gain muscular endurance, you have two choices. You can either extend the set by completing more repetitions or rest for a shorter amount of time between sets. Generally, a set of 12 to 20 reps should last at least 30 seconds but not more than 90 seconds. A prolonged set will encourage lactic acid buildup. This causes that familiar burning sensation and ultimately leads to fatigue.

Aim for one to three sets of 15 to 25 repetitions, resting for 30 to 60 seconds between sets. Another alternative is to perform three to five sets of 10 to 15 reps, resting for 15 to 30 seconds between sets.

Training for Muscular Strength

If strength is your goal, you need to use relatively heavy resistance to perform fewer repetitions per set. Rest for two to three minutes between sets. The goal of this type of training is to increase the overall strength of a muscle or group of muscles. Strength training usually includes exercises that work the major muscle groups, such as the bench press, seated row, and squat.

For best results, perform one to three sets of six to eight repetitions, resting for two and a half to three minutes between sets.

Training for Muscular Size

Many people who work out want to improve their overall appearance. Increasing muscle size is the number-one goal for most lifters. Hypertrophy is the technical term for building size, increasing mass, or bodybuilding. Despite popular myth, using very heavy weight as in strength training does not promote size increases as rapidly. Hypertrophy training falls somewhere between strength and endurance training. Training for hypertrophy involves a moderate number of reps with moderate to heavy weight and average rest periods.

The optimal way to increase size is to perform one to three sets of 8 to 12 repetitions (usually 10-12), resting for 90 seconds between sets.

Training for Power

Power training is explosive in nature and requires very quick movements using as much weight as possible while still lifting explosively. Only skilled lifters and sport-specific athletes should engage in power training. The true benefits of explosive training have not been satisfactorily demonstrated through research. Therefore, power training should not be attempted except under proper supervision. For true power development, light to moderate weight should be used.

Maximum Lifting

Maximum lifting implies heavy weights and only one to three repetitions per set. Maximum lifting is a good way to find your one-repetition maximum (1RM) but not a very good way to train. Before attempting to perform your max lift, practice proper lifting technique. This type of training is advantageous for power lifters or Olympic lifters but is not appropriate for general fitness enthusiasts or athletes. Furthermore, the rest time between sets needs to be so great that the workouts themselves have a low work output and require a long time to complete. A routine for training strength, hypertrophy, or endurance is better suited to most people.

Finding Your One-Repetition Maximum

For safety, use a spotter or a machine. If you use a machine, remember it will be 10 to 15 percent heavier than the free-weight version.

1. Perform one set of 10 reps with 50 percent of your estimated 1RM. Take a three-minute break.
2. Perform one set of five reps with 75 percent of your estimated 1RM. Take a three-minute break.
3. Perform one set of two reps with 85 to 90 percent of your estimated 1RM. Take a three-minute break.
4. Perform one set of one rep with 95 percent of your estimated 1RM. Take a three-minute break.
5. Add 5 to 10 pounds for one rep on each consecutive set, resting for three to five minutes between sets, until you can no longer perform the rep without help.

Types of Routines

To add variety and challenge to your basic program, try a few of the following modifications. Just as you can choose from different exercises and modes of resistance, you can choose from several different ways to train. Use the guidelines described in the following sections to determine reps and sets, the type of weight used, and the order of exercises. These are some of the more popular training methods.

Superset/Multiset

If you want an efficient workout that provides maximum benefit in minimum time, this is the method for you. In a superset, you perform two exercises one right after the other with little or no rest in between. (A multiset consists of more than two exercises.) This method has a distinct advantage in reducing overall exercise time and increasing muscle size, although it is not recommended if your primary goal is to develop strength.

Complete the first set of the first exercise, then move on to the next exercise without resting. The second exercise should work the opposite muscle group. For example, for a leg superset, begin with leg extensions, then move on to lying leg curls with no rest between sets. Essentially, you recover from the first exercise during the second exercise, although this recovery is not complete.

A multiset joins three or more exercises. For example, an arm multiset might include triceps pushdowns, dumbbell curls, and lateral raises. The longer you continue without rest, the more likely you will fatigue. If you are performing more than one superset or multiset, then rest for 60 to 120 seconds before beginning the next superset or multiset. Here are some popular superset groups:

- Leg superset: leg extension, lying leg curl
- Upper arm superset: supine triceps extension, dumbbell curl
- Upper back and shoulders superset: shoulder press, lat pulldown
- Upper back and chest superset: bench press, seated row

For each exercise, try two to three sets of 10 to 12 reps. For example, for the leg superset, you would perform a set of 10 to 12 leg extensions followed by a set of 10 to 12 lying leg curls, with no rest between exercises. Rest briefly before beginning the second set of leg extensions.

For some challenging multisets, check out the triple exhaust set in the appendix (page 123).

Circuit Training

Circuit training extends the multiset idea. All the exercises in a particular circuit follow one another with little rest. If you want to perform more than one circuit, rest three to five minutes between circuits. Circuits decrease time spent in the gym and increase muscular endurance. Hypertrophy will occur over time. You can alternate between upper and lower body exercises or between front and back exercises, or both.

See the appendix (page 122) for some great sample circuits, or you can create your own.

Preexhaust Training

As the name implies, in preexhaust training, the lifter forces a muscle or group of muscles to become exhausted before moving on to another exercise that works the same muscle. Begin with a single-joint, isolated exercise, one that moves about only one joint, then perform a double- or multijoint movement that works the same muscle group. Smaller muscles usually fatigue before larger ones, so the larger muscles in the multijoint movement are not entirely worked. The fatiguing smaller muscles usually cause the set to end early.

Although it sounds confusing, preexhaust training makes a lot of sense. Let's look at an example. Consider the typical weekend warrior or bodybuilder, who begins his chest routine with the bench press. Pecs are the major muscle group involved, but the triceps and front deltoids are worked as well. Since the weakest links in the bench press are the deltoids and triceps, they usually fatigue first. The weaker muscles lose their force capability, causing the end of the set to occur before the pecs have had a chance to break down completely. The net result is that the pecs don't reach complete exhaustion and require further concentrated exercises. So our warrior moves on to pec decks, cables, or another pec exercise, but he can't seem to get that maximum burn. The solution is preexhaust training. If nothing else, preexhaust training adds variety and challenge to the routine.

Here's how it works. Let's use the same two exercises (bench press and pec deck) but reverse the order and superset them. In other words, we preexhaust the pecs with a pec deck set to failure, then immediately follow it with a bench press. When our warrior finishes the set, his pecs should be adequately exhausted. Also, as he continues through the rest of his workout using preexhaust training, he will find his delts and triceps don't limit his pec workout. All three muscle groups receive an equal amount of torment.

Another variation of preexhaust training would be to complete all sets of the preexhaust exercise before moving on to the next exercise, rather than supersetting them. Both methods of preexhaust training are effective, but combined they can create even more variety.

Here are some of the most popular combinations:

■ Chest: dumbbell pec fly followed by bench press

- Upper back: dumbbell pullover followed by lat pulldown
- Shoulders and upper arms: supine triceps extension followed by shoulder press

Postexhaust Training

Postexhaust training is similar to preexhaust training except that the exhaustive movement follows the initial movement. A postexhaust exercise is usually a single-joint movement that isolates a particular muscle group. This movement follows a multijoint or main core movement.

The rationale behind this method of training is threefold. First, performing a postexhaust exercise immediately after a major movement increases the likelihood of overloading that particular muscle group, especially if a smaller stabilizer muscle limits maximal performance, as in the bench press example. Second, postexhaust training increases the ability to isolate a muscle or muscle group that needs the extra work, especially if it is hard to train or develop. Third, postexhaust exercises are a form of conditioning because the length of a normal set is extended by 30 seconds or more. This makes it a valuable method for muscular endurance training.

Here are some of the most popular combinations:

- Chest: bench press followed by pec fly
- Upper back: lat pulldown followed by dumbbell pullover
- Legs: leg press followed by leg extensions

Drop Sets

Drop refers to the act of decreasing resistance. Drop sets are often referred to as strip sets or burn sets. A drop set is performed as an extension of the initial set of the exercise. During the drop, resistance is removed by removing plates in free-weight exercises or lowering the weight in machine exercises. The lifter completes a prescribed number of reps to a point of relative failure, then the weight is immediately decreased and the lifter continues for another set of reps until failure. The number of drops varies depending on the goal of the exercise and the ability of the lifter to tolerate the pain. The drop should be about 20 percent of the initial weight each time, but it varies depending on the lifter's tolerance. Popular drop exercises are bench presses, rows, triceps exercises, biceps exercises, and leg extensions.

For example, if you started with 150 pounds for a bench press, you might perform one set of eight reps with the 150 pounds, then drop to 120 pounds, then to 90 pounds, and finally to 60 pounds. Starting with the 120 pounds, you should expect to do no more than four or five reps and possibly only one or two.

Negative Training

Negative training emphasizes the eccentric portion of the lift. The advantage of negative training is that the lifter can use more weight, causing the body to adapt to the increase in weight. The disadvantage is that it increases the risk of injury and requires a spotter. Negative training can be done with free weights or machines.

Negative training can be performed in two ways. In the first way, the lifter does a normal set until fatigued, then finishes with negative sets. The second way is called *negative emphasized.* As the name implies, the rep is normal except that the negative portion is exaggerated by increasing the time the lifter takes to lower the weight. In a negative rep, it should take at least five seconds to lower the weight. Any faster and the lifter is not truly working against the weight to slow it down. For negatives to work properly, the lifter needs to exert maximal force against the weight as if to push it up. If the amount of weight is correct, the lifter's maximal effort will still cause the weight to descend. If the weight is too heavy, the lifter's effort against it will not last long enough to create a benefit or the weight will just drop. If the weight is too light, the lifter will take too long to lower it. Too light a weight is not as bad as too heavy a weight.

By performing a normal set, then exhausting the muscles by performing additional negatives, the lifter gets more out of the set. This method works well because a person is as much as 20 to 40 percent stronger in the eccentric phase. The concentric movement will cause fatigue before the eccentric movement. Therefore, to achieve a good eccentric fatigued state, the negative portion can be worked for additional reps while the spotter helps the lifter during the concentric portion of the exercise.

Emphasized negatives are the most popular, safest, and most productive exercises, as they are controlled by the lifter. The lifter performs the normal concentric lift, then takes additional time to lower it. In other words, if the regular lifting cadence is two to three seconds concentric and three to four seconds eccentric, the new cadence would be two to three and six to eight seconds, respectively.

No matter which method of negative training you use, the result will be greater development from a single set and greater fatigue from eccentric exercise. The most popular exercises are the machine bench press, dumbbell curls, and leg extensions.

Forced Repetitions to Exhaustion

For forced repetitions, the lifter is forced to complete more reps than she can complete on her own. This method also prevents cheating while keeping the emphasis of the exercise and the tension on the specific muscle or muscle group. A spotter assists the lifter in performing the forced reps, but the spotter provides only a little help. If the spotter needs to help a lot, then the weight is too heavy or the set is over. This method is crucial for developing ultimate strength. Some good exercises for forced reps are the bench press, triceps extensions, biceps curls, leg extensions, and leg curls. Avoid forced reps with very technical lifts such as the squat and lunge.

Slow Training

There are several versions of slow training. In super slow training, the exercise is performed at a very slow pace, taking 30 to 60 seconds to complete a single repetition. Although advocates of super slow training believe it is a good method, there is little evidence to support this theory. Super slow training is difficult to perform and often boring, but there are other methods of slow training that provide both a strong stimulus for improvement and a great challenge.

A great method of slow training is to use a 5-second concentric phase followed by a 5- to 10-second eccentric phase of a single repetition. You can further enhance slow training by adding an isometric hold at the end of the concentric movement. Taking a leg curl as an example, perform a five-second concentric contraction, hold for five seconds at the top of the movement (fully contracted), then perform a five-second eccentric movement. Multiple reps can be performed (usually five). Slow training is good for developing both hypertrophy and muscular endurance.

Pyramid System

As the name implies, in pyramid training, the lifter increases or decreases the weight and/or reps. The weight changes between sets so that with each subsequent set, either the weight, the number of reps, or both increase or decrease according to the specific protocol.

There are three versions of this training with three kinds of pyramids, giving rise to nine different pyramid combinations. The major drawback with a pyramid is that the lifter has to save strength for later sets and therefore may never get in a truly good set. Figure 15.1 illustrates the possible pyramid scenarios.

To pyramid up, you can increase the weight and decrease the reps, increase the reps and decrease the weight, or increase both weight and reps. To pyramid down, decrease weight and increase reps, decrease reps and increase weight, or decrease both. For a real challenge, try pyramiding up and down. This can be done one of three ways: increase weight and decrease reps up, then decrease weight and increase reps down; increase reps and decrease weight up, then decrease reps and increase weight down; or increase both weight and reps up, then decrease both down.

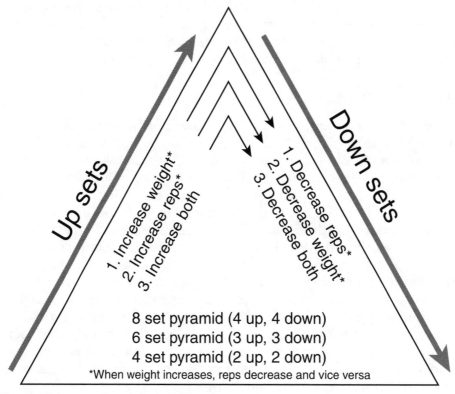

Figure 15.1 Pyramid combinations.

Concentration, or Blitz, System

In the concentration, or blitz, system, the entire workout is spent on a specific body part or movement so as to concentrate on that muscle or muscle group or movement. Sometimes as many as 6 sets are performed for each exercise and as many as 30 sets for the body part! For bodybuilders, this type of routine helps them focus on a weaker or smaller part, such as the biceps, that needs development. However, muscle group or body part concentration is not going to benefit an athlete training for sport performance. Training a specific movement or exercise may have merit if constant repetition of the same movement occurs during play. Concentration or blitz training typically requires several sessions per week to train the entire body and thus is not practical for the general population.

Here is a sample blitz training routine:

- Barbell curls 6 × 12
- Isolated biceps curls 6 × 12 each arm
- Preacher curls 6 × 12
- Cable curls 6 × 12

Remember, this is truly hard-core training. Extreme muscle soreness will occur in most people.

Split Training

In split training, certain muscles, muscle groups, or body parts become the focus. Almost all training, except for a full-body workout, uses some form of split training. If you split a workout for the upper body from a workout for the lower body, you create a split routine. You can take it a step further and split upper body (or lower body) exercises. For example, you may work chest, triceps, and shoulders one day and back and biceps another day.

Another variation of the split routine would be to split your workout into morning and evening sessions, perhaps working the lower body in the morning and the upper body in the evening. This can be effective if you have other demands on your time.

Split training is effective if your schedule allows a few more sessions per week in the weight room. Make split routines time-effective and goal-specific.

Advanced lifters perform more elaborate splits. Here are some common split routines:

- Upper body/lower body
- Chest, triceps, shoulders/back and biceps/legs

Push/Pull

Push/pull training incorporates split training, supersetting, or both. You may train push movements one day and pull the next day, or train both push and pull movements on the same day by alternating in the form of a superset or by resting between sets. You may complete an entire push exercise for all its prescribed sets before moving on to the pull exercise, or vice versa. For example, a lifter may do three sets of bench presses followed by three sets of seated rows.

This is a good method if time is an issue and you want to create muscular balance. Often lifters spend too much time working specific muscles and forget about the importance of muscle balance for avoiding injury.

SAMPLE PUSH/PULL ROUTINES

Push/pull 1
Bench press 2 × 10
Seated row 2 × 10
Shoulder/military press 2 × 10
Lat pulldown 2 × 10
Triceps pushdown 2 × 10
Biceps curl 2 × 10
Rest 90 seconds between sets

Push/pull 2
Perform circuit 2 to 3 times: Bench press 1 × 10 Seated row 1 × 10 Military press 1 × 10 Lat pulldown 1 × 10 Triceps pushdown 1 × 10
Biceps curl 1 × 10
Rest 60 seconds between sets

Putting Your Program Together

So, what should you do? The answer lies in the type of training program you want and the quality you are looking for.

Each training method requires different parameters with respect to sets, reps, and resistance. The fact that there are so many different training methods is ample proof that a training program is unique to the lifter. The key to figuring out what is best for you is to practice, using the sound principles discussed in the introduction. Work hard and use proper technique. The results you achieve are a function of the quality of the repetition and the degree of adaptation in your muscles.

If you are properly following the overload principle, the resistance should become difficult by the last one or two reps of the set. You can achieve your desired results by manipulating the number of sets and reps and the amount of rest.

Appendix

Sample Programs

With all the information you've learned in this book, you can create a weight training program specific to your goals, needs, and interests. Keep safety in mind. Training is challenging. Anything worth doing takes effort. Improving your health is one of those things. Don't overtrain or waste time. Train hard, train smart, but most important, train for fun.

Overall Body Workout

For most people, the overall total-body workout is the best choice. If you have a full schedule or do other physical activity, then this type of workout is for you. A total-body workout should take 30 to 60 minutes to complete. If you perform only one set per exercise, it may take less time. Remember, perform a good warm-up and stretch prior to beginning the workout.

When you do a total-body workout, your individual results from split routine and isolated work will decrease but your overall results will be better. You should lift weights before other activity such as aerobics if your primary goal is to improve muscle strength and size. For general health, however, it doesn't matter which you do first.

General Workout

This is the standard workout that most health club and general fitness enthusiasts advocate. Perform each exercise for two sets of 12 repetitions.

Bench press

Machine pec fly

Shoulder press

Seated row

Triceps pushdown

Dumbbell curl

Leg press

Leg extension

Lying leg curl

Heel raise

Total-Body Supercircuit

Perform each exercise for one set of 12 repetitions. Perform the exercises in order, with minimal rest between them—only enough to set up the next machine. When the circuit is complete, take a breather for about two minutes, then attempt a second circuit. If you feel especially good, try a third circuit. You may choose one of the three circuits, or you can do all three. If you choose to do more than one circuit on a particular day, go through each circuit only once.

SUPER CIRCUITS

Circuit 1	Circuit 2	Circuit 3
Bench press	Bench press	Lunge
Leg press	Seated row	Incline bench press
Seated row	Shoulder press	Leg press
Lying leg curl	Dumbbell curl	Lat pulldown
Shoulder press	Triceps pushdown	Single-leg curl
Leg extension	Leg press	Lateral raise
Triceps pushdown	Seated leg curl	Heel raise
Heel raise	Leg extension	Supine triceps extension
Dumbbell curl	Heel raise	Toe pull
Seated calf	Seated calf	Dumbbell curl
Curl-up	Curl-up	Ab circuit: Curl-up 1 × 15 Twisting curl-up 1 × 15 each side Pelvic raise 1 × 15
Back extension	Back extension	

Preexhaust or Postexhaust Routine

In this challenging routine, the first exercise should use 10 to 12 repetitions and the second exercise 8 to 10 with no rest between each pair. Take a 90-second rest before attempting the next pair. You may alternate upper and lower body exercises or perform the upper, then the lower. You don't need to do more than two sets of each pair because, if executed properly, you will get a very good workout. Be careful on the triple set exhaust.

PRE- AND POSTEXHAUST ROUTINES

Double Exhaust		Triple Exhaust	
Preexhaust	Postexhaust	Preexhaust	Postexhaust
Dumbbell pec fly* Bench press	Bench press Dumbbell pec fly*	Dumbbell pec fly* Bench press Cable cross	Bench press Dumbbell pec fly* Incline bench press
Leg extension Leg press	Leg press Leg extension	Leg extension Leg press Leg extension	Leg press Leg extension Leg press
Dumbbell pullover Lat pulldown	Lat pulldown Dumbbell pullover	Dumbbell pullover Lat pulldown Dumbbell pullover	Lat pulldown Dumbbell pullover Lat pulldown
Heel raise Lying leg curl	Lying leg curl Heel raise	Heel raise Lying leg curl Seated calf	Lying leg curl Heel raise Seated leg curl
Supine triceps extension Shoulder press	Shoulder press Lateral raise	Supine triceps extension Shoulder press Supine triceps extension	Shoulder press Lateral raise Shoulder press
Curl-up Back extension	Curl-up Back extension	Curl-up Back extension	Curl-up Back extension

*The machine pec fly may be used instead of the dumbbell pec fly.

Body Weight Workout

One of the best ways to get into shape and challenge yourself is to use your own body weight as resistance. This is also a perfect way to exercise in your hotel room on vacation, out on the field of play, or just for a good change from the ordinary. Perform each exercise for two sets of 12 repetitions. Take 60-second breaks between exercises. Change the order of the exercises for more variety. If you are up for a bigger challenge, try three sets of 15 reps of each exercise with only 30-second breaks between sets. Watch out—this may be more difficult than it looks.

Lunge

Squat

Straight-leg deadlift with hands on head (using body weight instead of the barbell)

Single-leg heel raise

Diamond push-up (position hands close together, forming a diamond shape with your thumbs and forefingers)

Normal or wide-hand push-up (position hands more than shoulder-width apart)

Dip

Front pull or chin-up

Curl-up

Split Routines

Splits are the most popular way to work out. They are more challenging and help isolate specific areas. For the split to be effective, you should work out at least two times a week. Advanced bodybuilders may work out as many as six times a week, but to stay safe and prevent overtraining, don't plan more than four weight training sessions a week.

With split routines, you need to respect the 24 to 48 hours of rest your muscles need before you work the next muscle group.

Standard Split

Probably the most popular split and most common workout week includes two upper body days and one leg day. Exercises can be performed with machines, barbells, or dumbbells. Incorporating pre- or postexhaust routines, negative routines, or slow training techniques will add even greater challenge.

Isolated shoulder work is optional. On both day 1 and day 2, the anterior, medial, and posterior heads of the shoulders will work. If you really want to work your shoulders, do it on day 1. You can add shoulder presses after the dumbbell presses. Some people work the shoulders on day 3 as additional work and do both the shoulder press and lateral raise for three sets of 10 to 12 reps each. Adding shoulders on day 3 makes for a long, difficult workout and should be done only after you have been training for some time.

THREE-DAY SPLIT ROUTINE

Day 1 Chest and triceps	Day 2 Back and biceps	Day 3 Legs
Bench press 3 × 8 to 10	Chin-up 2 × 12	Squat 3 × 10
Incline bench press 2 × 8 to 10	Lat pulldown 3 × 8 to 10	Leg press 3 × 10
Dumbbell bench press 2 × 8	Seated row 2 × 8 to 10	Leg extension 3 × 10
Dumbbell pec fly 3 × 12	Dumbbell row 2 × 8	Straight-leg deadlift 2 × 10
Dip 3 × 10 to 15	Straight bar curl 3 × 12	Seated leg curl 3 × 12
Supine triceps extension 3 × 12	Preacher curl 3 × 12	Heel raise 3 × 12
Triceps pushdown 2 × 10	Dumbbell curl 2 × 8	Seated calf 3 × 12
Curl-up 2 × 15	Curl-up 2 × 15	Curl-up 2 × 15

Two-Day Repeat

This workout is designed for the person who likes to work out and challenge the body to work overtime. Twice a week, you will add leg work on either day 1 or day 2, but not both.

TWO-DAY REPEAT WORKOUT

Day 1 Push exercises	Day 2 Pull exercises
Bench press 3 × 8	Seated row 3 × 8
Incline bench press 3 × 8	Lat pulldown 3 × 8
Shoulder press 2 × 8	Lat pulldown with palms turned in 2 × 8
Dip 2 × 10	Straight bar curl 2 × 10
Machine pec fly 2 × 10	Preacher curl 2 × 10
Supine triceps extension 2 × 10	Dumbbell curl 2 × 10
Triceps pushdown 2 × 10	Curl-up 3 × 12
Lateral raise 2 × 10	

To either day 1 or day 2 (but not both), add the traditional leg routine:
- Leg press 3 × 8 to 12
- Leg extension 3 × 8 to 12
- Lying leg curl 3 × 8 to 12
- Heel raise 3 × 8 to 12

Five-Day Split and Six-Day "I Am a Maniac" Split

These routines are for highly advanced lifters; they are too much training for those looking for general and sport-specific fitness. Other than competitive bodybuilders and strength athletes, lifters should avoid these workouts. These advanced splits alternate the days for the two-day repeat and standard splits.

SIX-DAY SPLIT ROUTINE

Pecs	Upper back
Bench press 4 × 12	Lat pulldown with palms turned in 4 × 12
Incline bench press 4 × 10	Lat pulldown 4 × 12
Dumbbell pec fly 4 × 12	Cable seated row 4 × 10
Cable cross 4 × 10	Machine seated row 4 × 10
Dumbbell bench press 4 × 10	Dumbbell row 4 × 10
	Ab circuit: Curl-up 2 × 12 Twisting curl-up 1 × 15 each side Pelvic raise 1 × 15

Shoulders and traps	Quads
Shoulder press 4 × 12	Squat 4 × 12
Front raise 4 × 12	Leg press 4 × 12
Lateral raise 4 × 12	Lunge 4 × 12
Rear deltoid fly 4 × 12	Leg extension 4 × 12
Shoulder shrug 4 × 12	Ab circuit: Curl-up 2 × 12 Twisting curl-up 1 × 15 each side Pelvic raise 1 × 15
Upright row 4 × 12	

Triceps and hams	Biceps and calves
Supine triceps extension 4 × 12	Straight bar curl 4 × 12
Triceps pushdown 4 × 12	Preacher curl 4 × 12
Dip 4 × 12	Dumbbell curl 4 × 12
Straight-leg deadlift 4 × 12	Heel raise 4 × 12
Seated leg curl 4 × 12	Seated calf 4 × 12
	Ab circuit (two sets of each exercise): Curl-up 1 × 15 Twisting curl-up 1 × 15 each side Pelvic raise 1 × 15

In the five-day split, the lifter may alternate day 1 and day 2 twice and have one day 3. Alternatively, the lifter may just continually cycle days, making every week different. In other words, day 1 may be Monday and Thursday in the first week, but won't be Monday and Thursday again for three weeks.

The six-day split repeats the standard split twice or the two-day repeat three grueling times. Alternatively, if lifters want to work out six days a week on weights, they might opt to work each body part individually. The table shows some individual body part training routines.

Again, this routine is for advanced lifters looking for specific gains. Inevitably, this type of training will lead to overtraining if proper rest and experience are not considered.

Challenge Yourself

If you get bored with your usual routine, try one of the following programs. These programs are designed to add variety and provide a challenge. They are specific routines with a given set of instructions. Of course, these routines can be modified to fit your needs or your imagination.

Leg-Acy

This routine will leave a lasting impression. Continue reps until failure, and always use perfect technique.

First set: count one second up, two seconds down for each rep; no rest between exercises.

- Leg extension 1 × 10
- Seated leg curl 1 × 10

Rest 90 seconds.

Second set: use 1/2 to 3/4 the amount of weight used in the first set; count five seconds up, five seconds hold, five seconds down for each rep; maintain form and time for the entire set; no rest between exercises.

- Leg extension 1 × 5
- Seated leg curl 1 × 5

Rest 90 seconds.

Third set: negative training; use 1 1/4 to 1 1/2 times the amount of weight used in the first set; spotter lifts weight to top position, then lifter lowers it using a four count.

- Leg extension 1 × 6
- Seated leg curl 1 × 6

Rest three minutes.

Fourth set: no rest between exercises; count two seconds up, three seconds down.

- Adductor cable lift 1 × 12
- Side cable lift 1 × 12
- Butt blasters 1 × 12 (if a good butt blaster machine is available; otherwise, skip this exercise)
- Lunge 1 × 12 each leg

Rest two minutes.

Fifth set: no rest between exercises; count two seconds up, three seconds down.

- Lunge 1 × 12
- Adductor cable lift 1 × 12
- Side cable lift 1 × 12
- Butt blasters 1 × 12 (if good butt blaster machine is available; otherwise, skip this exercise)

Rest three minutes. Repeat either the fourth or fifth set if you need the work.

Sixth set: no rest between exercises; count two seconds up, three seconds down on each rep; if you do not reach failure at the tenth rep, use more weight.

- Heel raise 1 × 10
- Seated calf 1 × 10

Rest 30 to 60 seconds.

Seventh set: no rest between exercises; count two seconds up, three seconds down on each rep; if you do not reach failure at the tenth rep, use more weight.

- Heel raise 1 × 10
- Seated calf 1 × 10

If you need more calf work, you can repeat the sixth and seventh supersets.

Tug o' War

This routine is a push/pull nightmare that will leave you exhausted without the rope burn.

First set: begin with a weight with which you can perform 10 reps; count two seconds up, four seconds hold, two seconds down for each rep.

- Bench press 1 × 6
- Seated row 1 × 6
- Shoulder press 1 × 6
- Lat pulldown 1 × 6
- Triceps pushdown 1 × 6
- Cable curl 1 × 6

Second set: use 1/3 the amount of weight used in the first set; count two seconds up, four seconds hold, two seconds down for each rep.

- Bench press 1 × 6
- Seated row 1 × 6
- Shoulder press 1 × 6
- Lat pulldown 1 × 6
- Triceps pushdown 1 × 6
- Cable curl 1 × 6

Rest two minutes.

Third set: use 1/3 the amount of weight used in the second set; count two seconds up, four seconds hold, two seconds down for each rep.

- Bench press 1 × 6
- Seated row 1 × 6
- Shoulder press 1 × 6
- Lat pulldown 1 × 6
- Triceps pushdown 1 × 6
- Cable curl 1 × 6

Rest three minutes, then repeat the third set.
Rest five minutes.

Fourth set: this superset will exhaust the muscle going into the fifth set, so choose your weight carefully.

- Dumbbell pec fly 1 × 10
- Dumbbell bench press 1 × 10

Rest 60 seconds.

Fifth set: this superset will exhaust the muscle going into the sixth set, so choose your weight carefully.

- Rear deltoid fly 1 × 10
- Dumbbell row 1 × 10

Rest 60 seconds.

Sixth set: Your muscle should feel a bit fatigued by now; choose your weight carefully and go for it!

- Dumbbell triceps kickback 1 × 10
- Dumbbell curl 1 × 10

Rest three minutes, then repeat the fourth, fifth, and sixth sets.

Dumbbell Complex

Dumbbells are a great way to add variation to your routine. The movement is the same, although you will need to watch your form and keep your body stable.

Here is a truly challenging routine. This supercircuit pulls out all the stops.

First circuit

- Dumbbell bench press 1 × 12
- Dumbbell bent-over row 1 × 12
- Dumbbell overhead press 1 × 12
- Dumbbell upright row 1 × 12
- Dumbbell triceps kickback or overhead kickback 1 × 12
- Dumbbell curl 1 × 12
- Squats with dumbbells held at shoulders 1 × 12
- Dumbbell straight-leg deadlifts 1 × 12
- Single-leg heel raise with dumbbells hanging at sides 1 × 12
- Curl-ups with dumbbells held at shoulders 1 × 12

Second circuit

- Dumbbell bench press 1 × 12
- Squats with dumbbells held at shoulders 1 × 12
- Dumbbell bent-over row 1 × 12
- Dumbbell straight-leg deadlifts 1 × 12
- Dumbbell overhead press 1 × 12
- Single-leg heel raise with dumbbells hanging at sides 1 × 12
- Dumbbell upright row 1 × 12
- Curl-ups with dumbbells held at shoulders 1 × 12
- Dumbbell triceps kickback or overhead kickback 1 × 12
- Dumbbell curl 1 × 12

Third circuit: supersets; perform the first rep of the first movement, then perform the first rep of the second movement.

- Squats with dumbbells held at shoulders/dumbbell overhead press 1 × 12
- Dumbbell straight-leg deadlifts/dumbbell upright row 1 × 12
- Dumbbell bench press/dumbbell kickbacks or overhead kickbacks 1 × 12
- Dumbbell bent-over row/dumbbell curl 1 × 12
- Single-leg heel raise with dumbbells hanging at sides/curl-ups with dumbbells held at shoulders 1 × 12

About the Writer

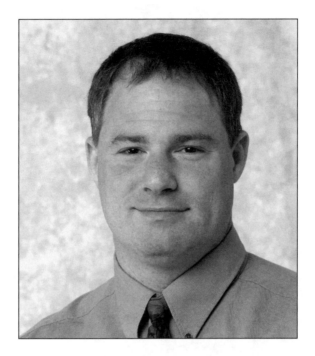

David Sandler is a professor of kinesiology at Florida International University, where he teaches strength training and biomechanics courses. Sandler is also a PhD candidate and research associate at the University of Miami, where he was a strength coach and held national records in the bench press. He is a frequent contributor to magazines such as *Muscle and Fitness*, *American Men's Health*, *Men's Health*, and *Oxygen*. Sandler serves as a faculty, board, and committee member for several national fitness organizations, including the National Strength and Conditioning Association.

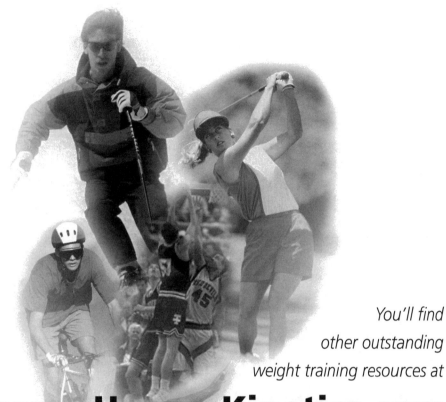